WHAT'S FEAR GOT TO DO WITH IT?

What's Fear Got to Do With It?

First Edition

ISBN 978-1-77262-088-7

Printed by Gauvin in Gatineau, Quebec, Canada

Conundrum Press
Wolfville, NS
www.conundrumpress.com

Although sometimes inspired by real people and events, all characters and incidents in this book are fictional.

A much shorter version of this story appeared in the self-published book *Where have you been?* It won a Doug Wright Award in 2023.

Conundrum Press acknowledges the financial support of the Canada Council for the Arts, the province of Nova Scotia and the government of Canada toward its publishing activities.

The author acknowledges the support of the Canada Council for the Arts in the creation of this work.

NOVA SCOTIA Canada

Canada Council for the Arts
Conseil des Arts du Canada

Ivana Filipovich

WHAT'S FEAR GOT TO DO WITH IT?

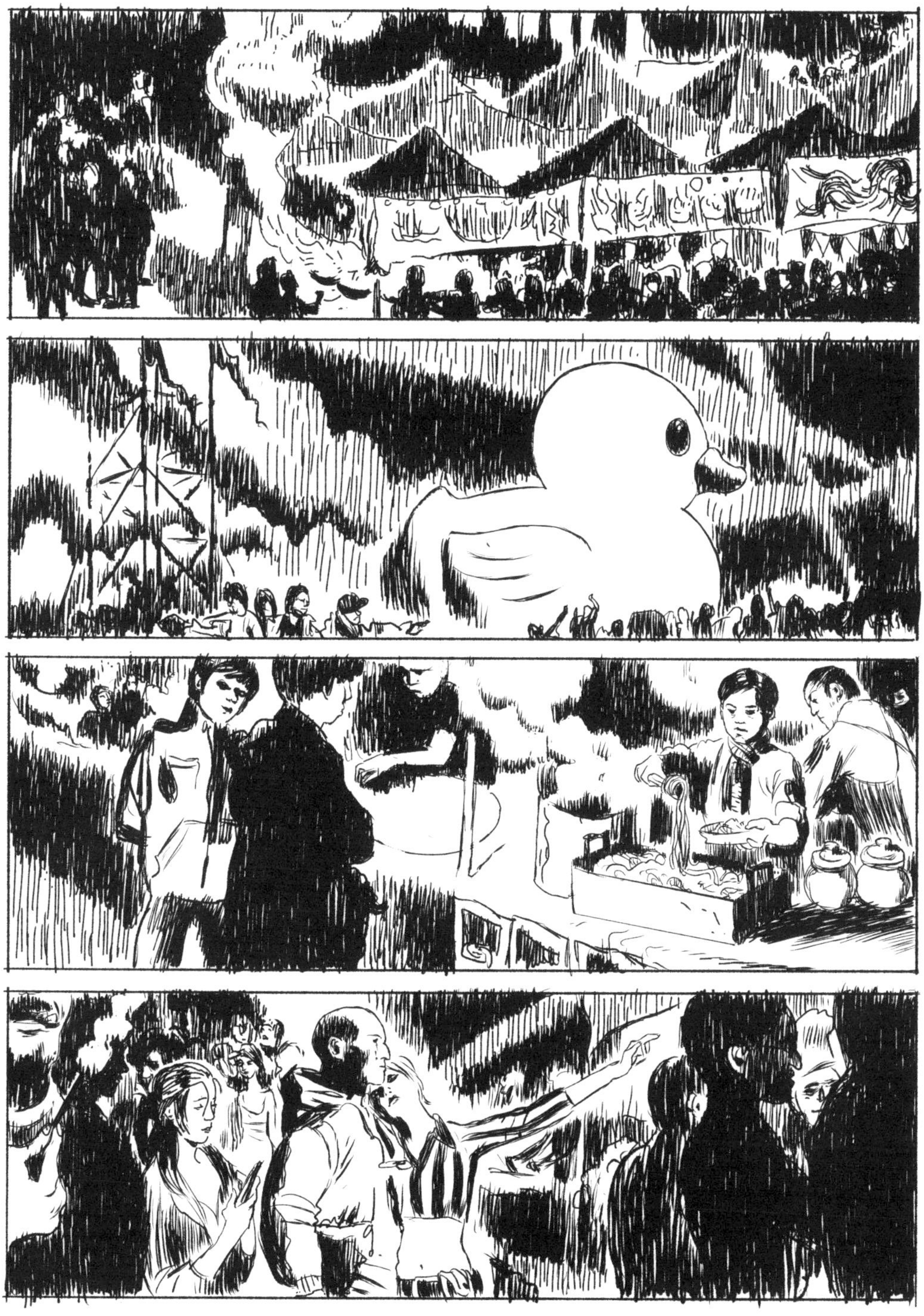

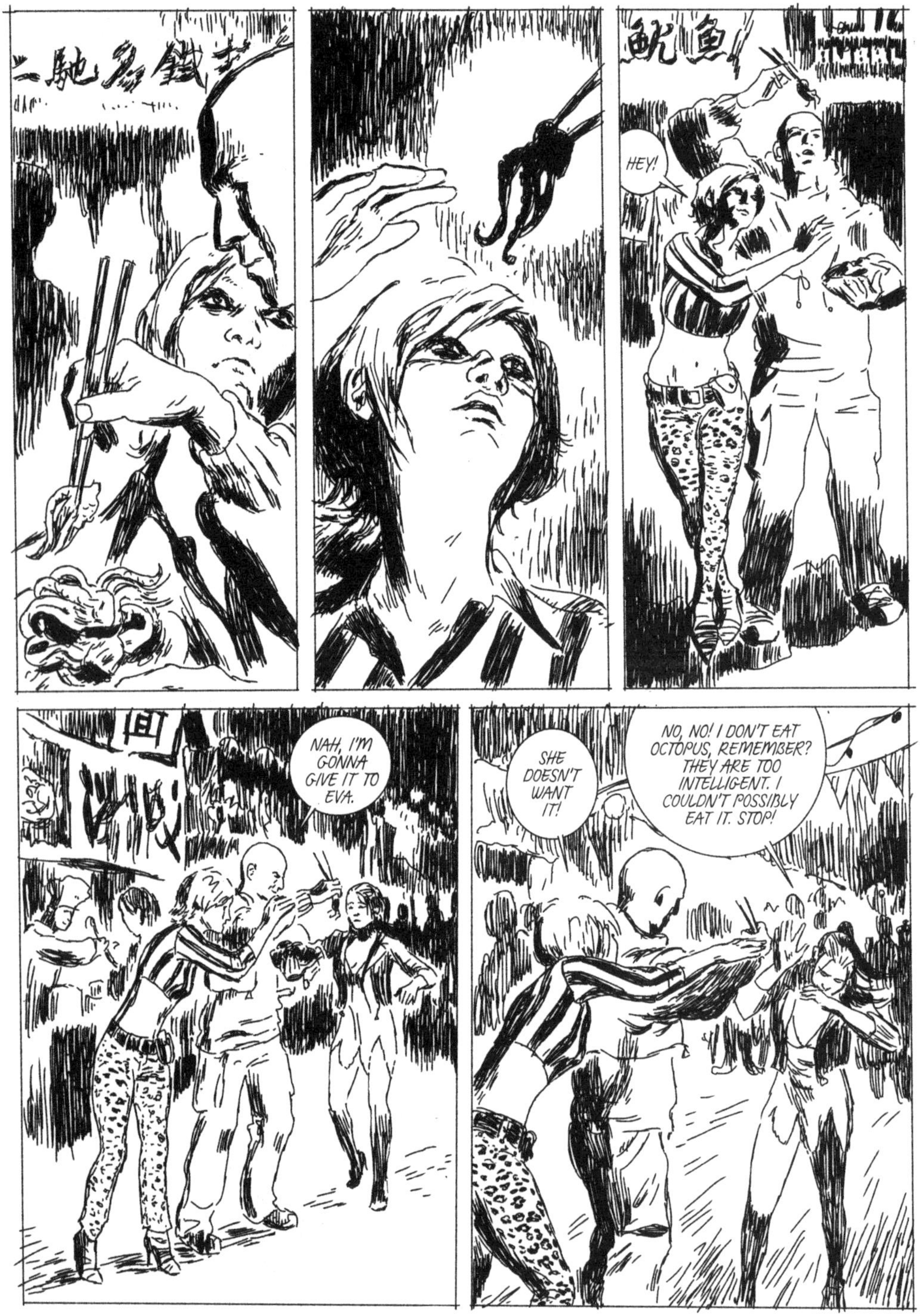
HEY!
NAH, I'M GONNA GIVE IT TO EVA.
SHE DOESN'T WANT IT!
NO, NO! I DON'T EAT OCTOPUS, REMEMBER? THEY ARE TOO INTELLIGENT. I COULDN'T POSSIBLY EAT IT. STOP!

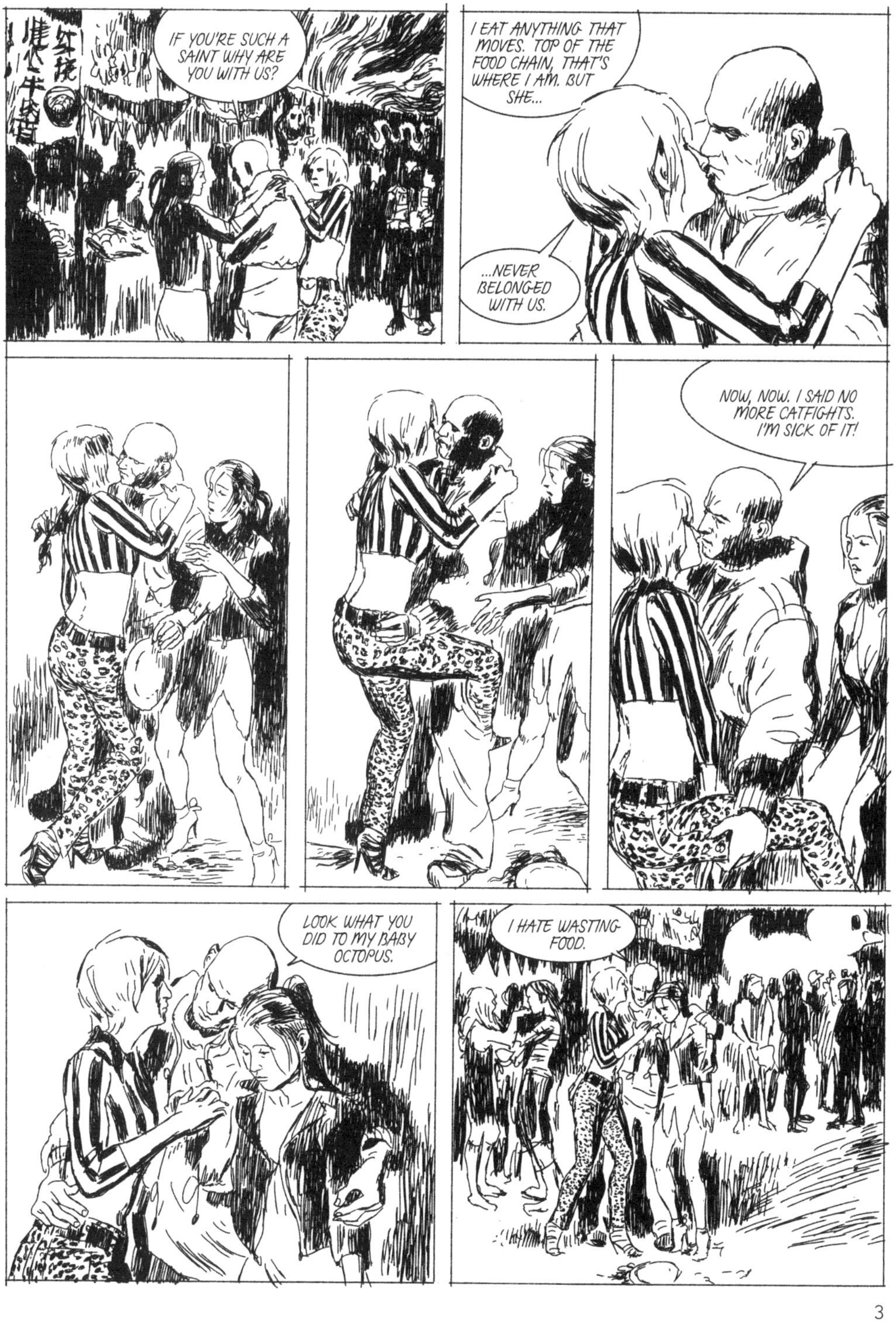
IF YOU'RE SUCH A SAINT WHY ARE YOU WITH US?
I EAT ANYTHING THAT MOVES. TOP OF THE FOOD CHAIN, THAT'S WHERE I AM. BUT SHE...
...NEVER BELONGED WITH US.
NOW, NOW. I SAID NO MORE CATFIGHTS. I'M SICK OF IT!
LOOK WHAT YOU DID TO MY BABY OCTOPUS.
I HATE WASTING FOOD.

SHIT!

EVA, TAKE A PHOTO QUICK! I NEED TO POST SOMETHING ON INSTAGRAM.

WHY DON'T YOU USE BUFFER TO SCHEDULE POSTS? THAT'S WHAT WE USE AT WORK AT THE GALLERY.

NO WAY! MY FOLLOWERS WOULD KNOW. IT HAS TO BE SPONTANEOUS. THAT'S WHAT THEY LIKE ABOUT ME.

LOOK AT ME, MR. NATURAL.

THIS SHOT IS FUCKING GARBAGE!

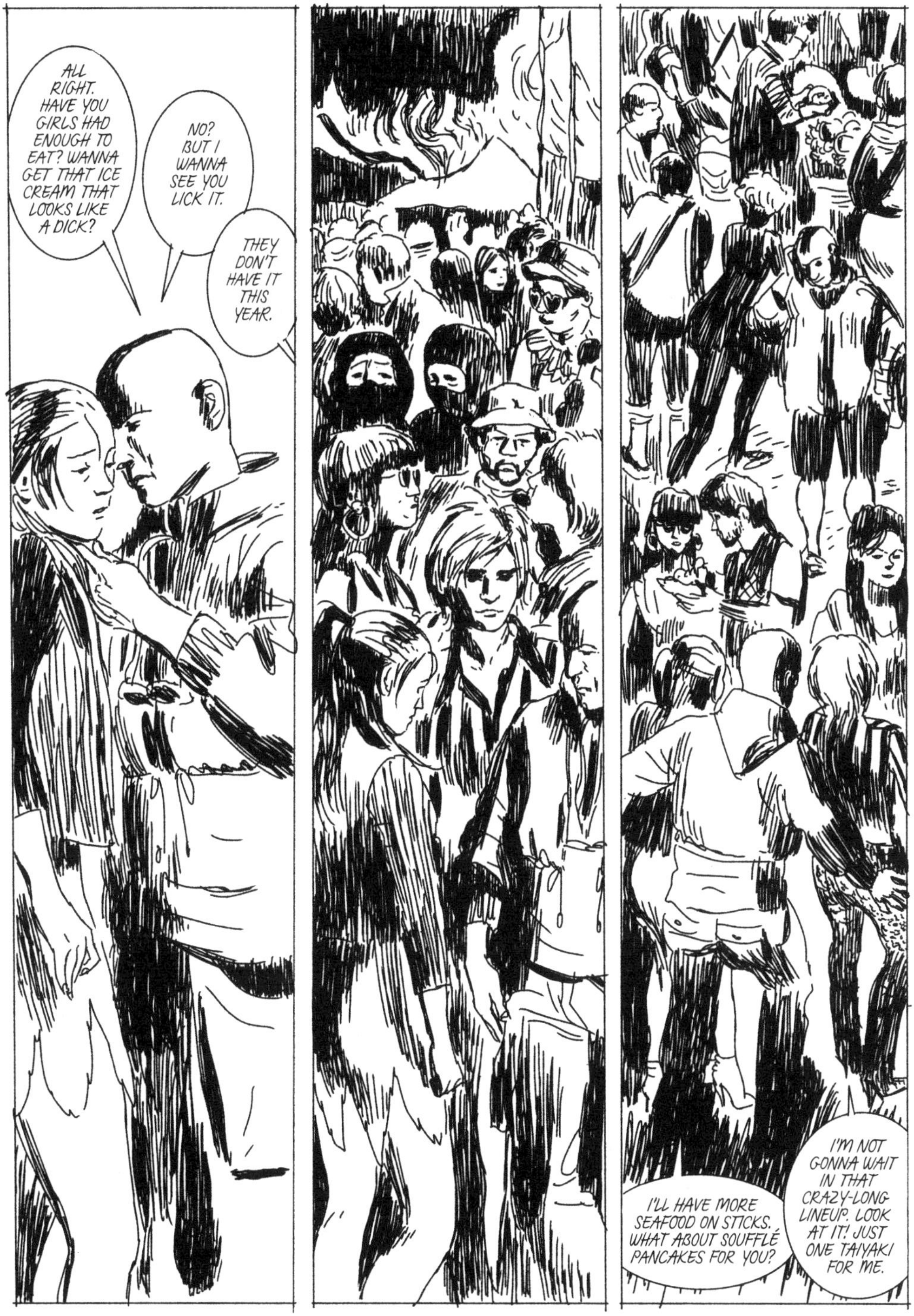
ALL RIGHT. HAVE YOU GIRLS HAD ENOUGH TO EAT? WANNA GET THAT ICE CREAM THAT LOOKS LIKE A DICK?
NO? BUT I WANNA SEE YOU LICK IT.
THEY DON'T HAVE IT THIS YEAR.
I'LL HAVE MORE SEAFOOD ON STICKS. WHAT ABOUT SOUFFLÉ PANCAKES FOR YOU?
I'M NOT GONNA WAIT IN THAT CRAZY-LONG LINEUP. LOOK AT IT! JUST ONE TAIYAKI FOR ME.

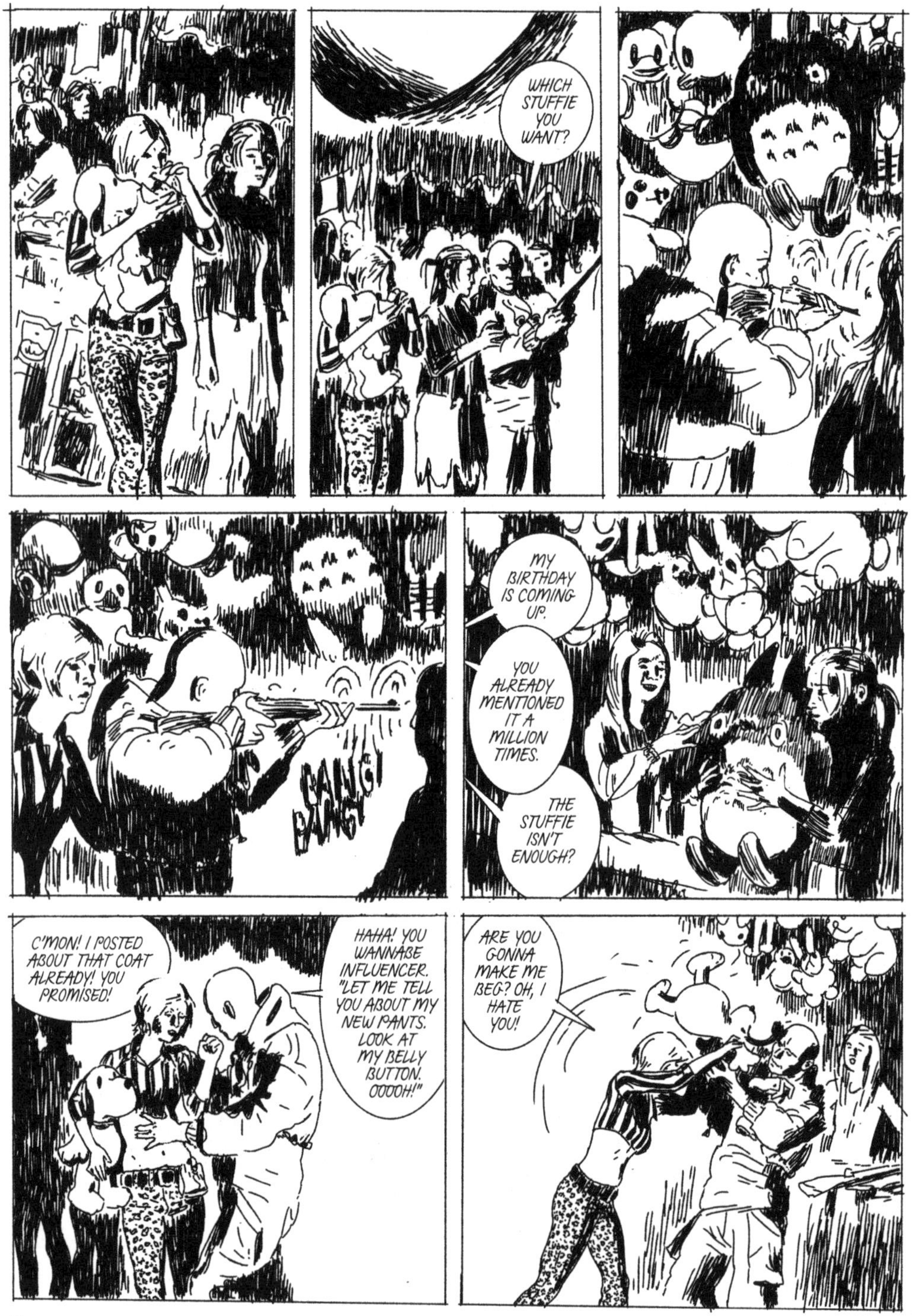
WHICH STUFFIE YOU WANT?
BANG! BANG!
MY BIRTHDAY IS COMING UP.
YOU ALREADY MENTIONED IT A MILLION TIMES.
THE STUFFIE ISN'T ENOUGH?
C'MON! I POSTED ABOUT THAT COAT ALREADY! YOU PROMISED!
HAHA! YOU WANNABE INFLUENCER. "LET ME TELL YOU ABOUT MY NEW PANTS. LOOK AT MY BELLY BUTTON. OOOOH!"
ARE YOU GONNA MAKE ME BEG? OH, I HATE YOU!

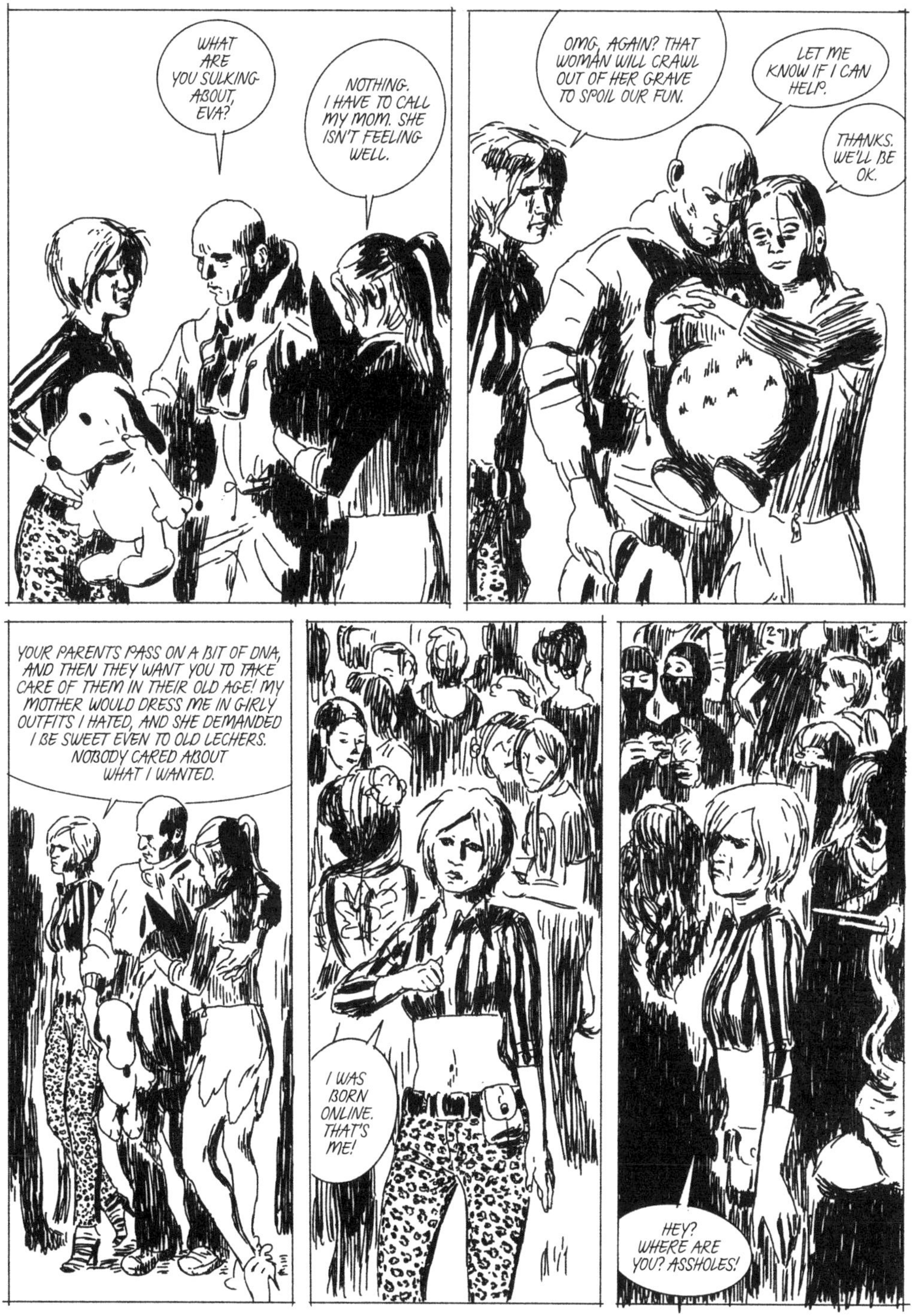
WHAT ARE YOU SULKING ABOUT, EVA?
NOTHING. I HAVE TO CALL MY MOM. SHE ISN'T FEELING WELL.
OMG, AGAIN? THAT WOMAN WILL CRAWL OUT OF HER GRAVE TO SPOIL OUR FUN.
LET ME KNOW IF I CAN HELP.
THANKS. WE'LL BE OK.
YOUR PARENTS PASS ON A BIT OF DNA, AND THEN THEY WANT YOU TO TAKE CARE OF THEM IN THEIR OLD AGE! MY MOTHER WOULD DRESS ME IN GIRLY OUTFITS I HATED, AND SHE DEMANDED I BE SWEET EVEN TO OLD LECHERS. NOBODY CARED ABOUT WHAT I WANTED.
I WAS BORN ONLINE. THAT'S ME!
HEY? WHERE ARE YOU? ASSHOLES!

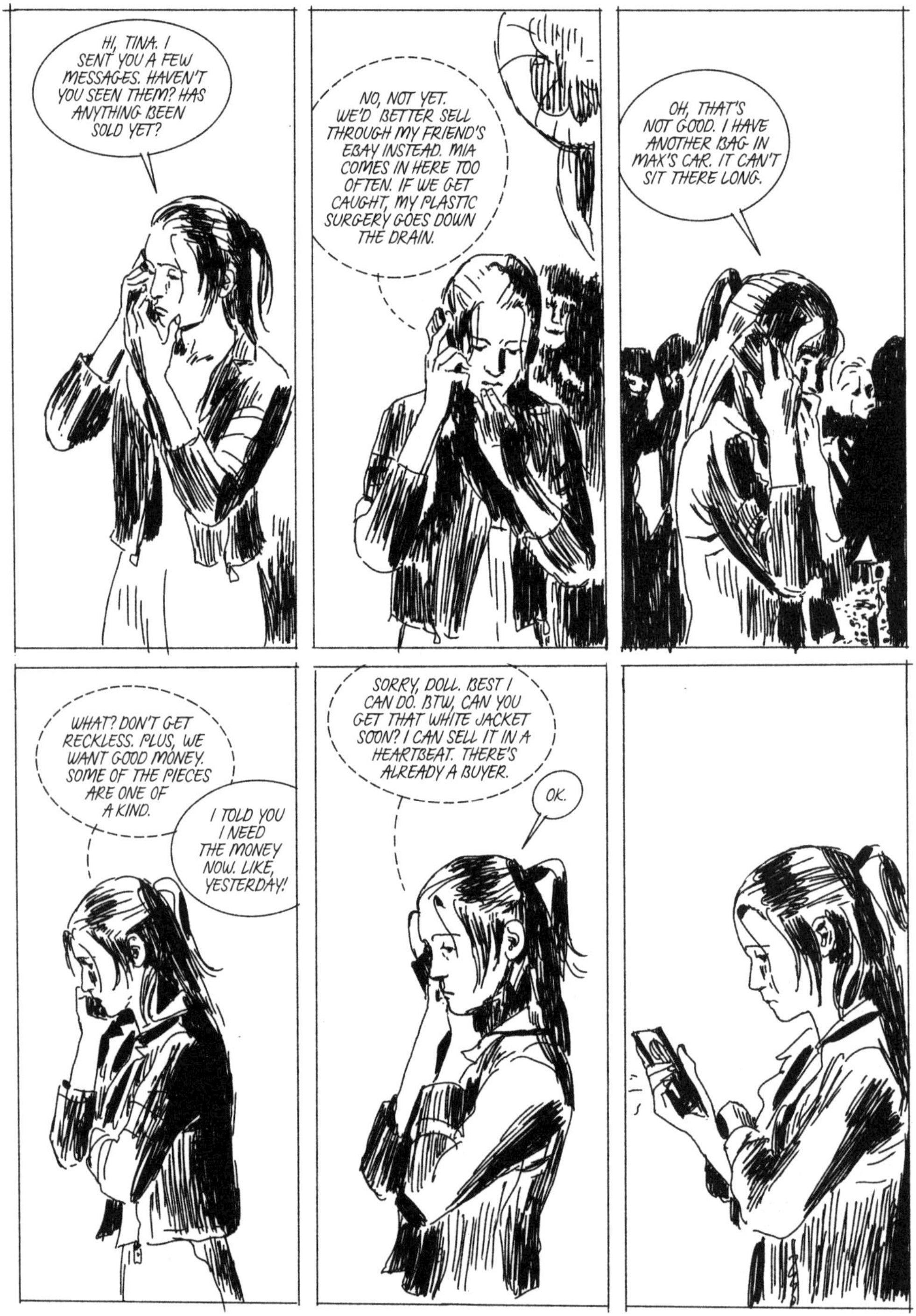
HI, TINA. I SENT YOU A FEW MESSAGES. HAVEN'T YOU SEEN THEM? HAS ANYTHING BEEN SOLD YET?
NO, NOT YET. WE'D BETTER SELL THROUGH MY FRIEND'S EBAY INSTEAD. MIA COMES IN HERE TOO OFTEN. IF WE GET CAUGHT, MY PLASTIC SURGERY GOES DOWN THE DRAIN.
OH, THAT'S NOT GOOD. I HAVE ANOTHER BAG IN MAX'S CAR. IT CAN'T SIT THERE LONG.
WHAT? DON'T GET RECKLESS. PLUS, WE WANT GOOD MONEY. SOME OF THE PIECES ARE ONE OF A KIND.
I TOLD YOU I NEED THE MONEY NOW. LIKE, YESTERDAY!
SORRY, DOLL. BEST I CAN DO. BTW, CAN YOU GET THAT WHITE JACKET SOON? I CAN SELL IT IN A HEARTBEAT. THERE'S ALREADY A BUYER.
OK.

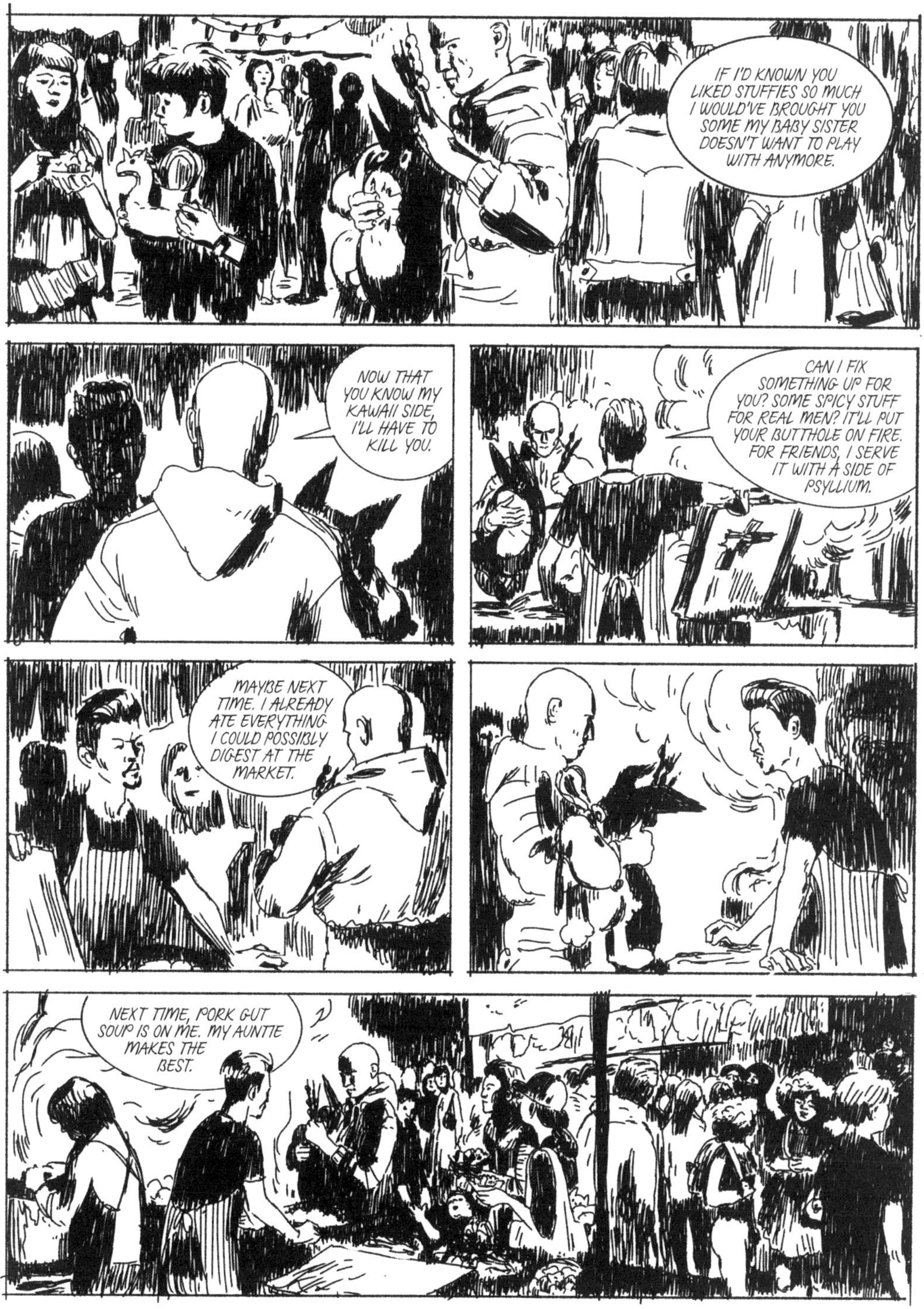
IF I'D KNOWN YOU LIKED STUFFIES SO MUCH I WOULD'VE BROUGHT YOU SOME MY BABY SISTER DOESN'T WANT TO PLAY WITH ANYMORE.
NOW THAT YOU KNOW MY KAWAII SIDE, I'LL HAVE TO KILL YOU.
CAN I FIX SOMETHING UP FOR YOU? SOME SPICY STUFF FOR REAL MEN? IT'LL PUT YOUR BUTTHOLE ON FIRE. FOR FRIENDS, I SERVE IT WITH A SIDE OF PSYLLIUM.
MAYBE NEXT TIME. I ALREADY ATE EVERYTHING I COULD POSSIBLY DIGEST AT THE MARKET.
NEXT TIME, PORK GUT SOUP IS ON ME. MY AUNTIE MAKES THE BEST.

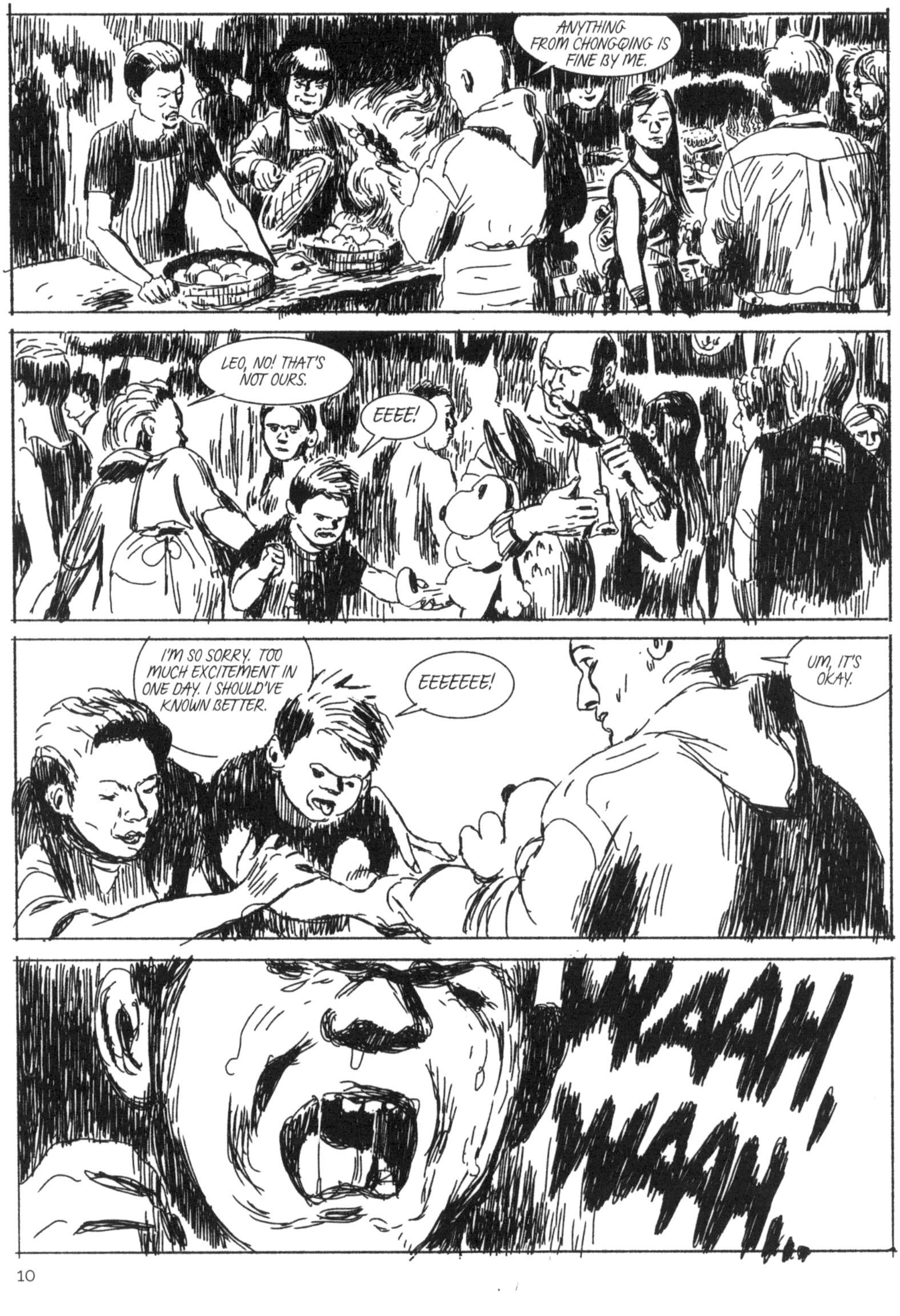
ANYTHING FROM CHONGQING IS FINE BY ME.
LEO, NO! THAT'S NOT OURS.
EEEE!
I'M SO SORRY. TOO MUCH EXCITEMENT IN ONE DAY. I SHOULD'VE KNOWN BETTER.
EEEEEEE!
UM, IT'S OKAY.
WAAH WAAH WAAH...

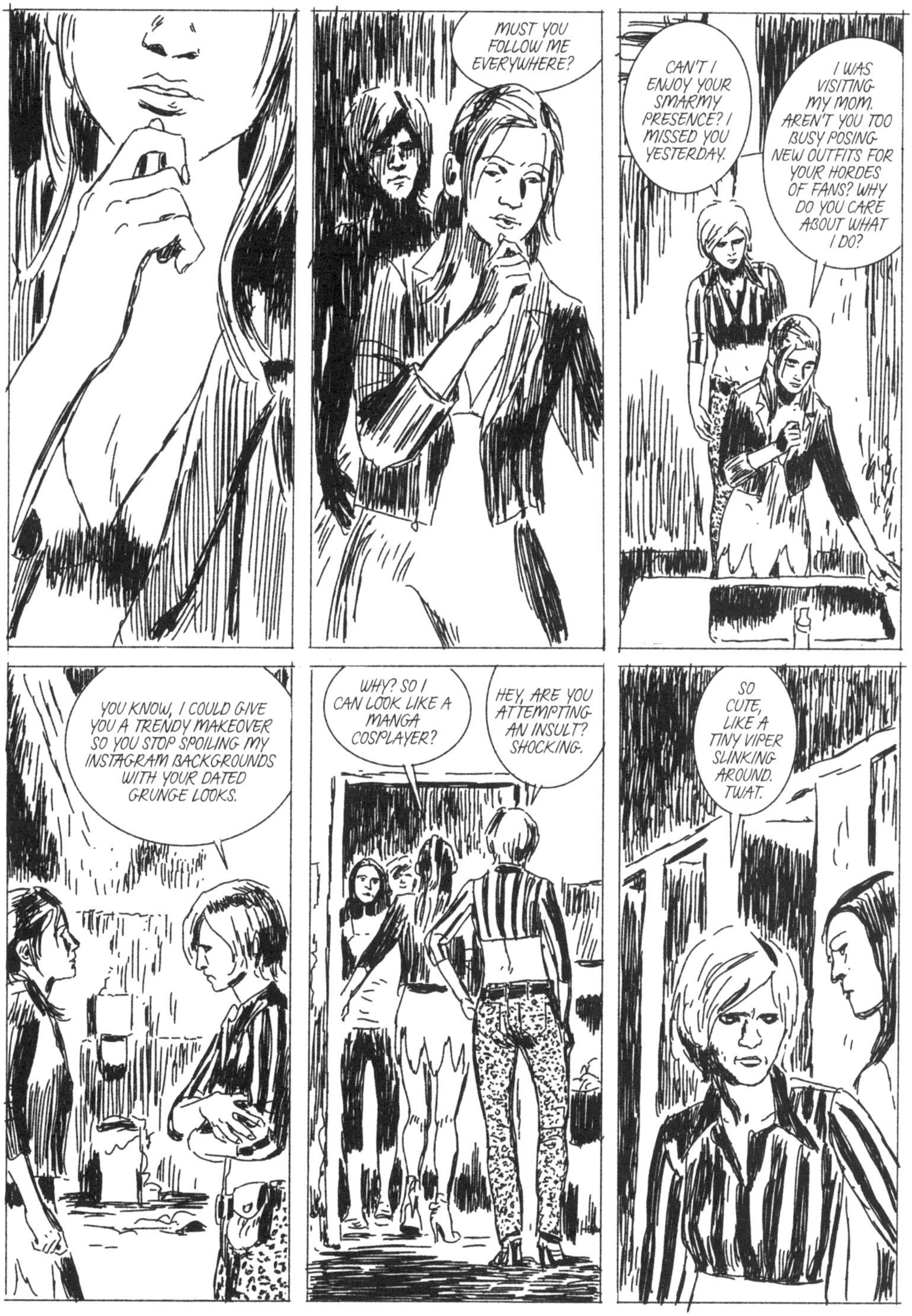
MUST YOU FOLLOW ME EVERYWHERE?
CAN'T I ENJOY YOUR SMARMY PRESENCE? I MISSED YOU YESTERDAY.
I WAS VISITING MY MOM. AREN'T YOU TOO BUSY POSING NEW OUTFITS FOR YOUR HORDES OF FANS? WHY DO YOU CARE ABOUT WHAT I DO?
YOU KNOW, I COULD GIVE YOU A TRENDY MAKEOVER SO YOU STOP SPOILING MY INSTAGRAM BACKGROUNDS WITH YOUR DATED GRUNGE LOOKS.
WHY? SO I CAN LOOK LIKE A MANGA COSPLAYER?
HEY, ARE YOU ATTEMPTING AN INSULT? SHOCKING.
SO CUTE, LIKE A TINY VIPER SLINKING AROUND. TWAT.

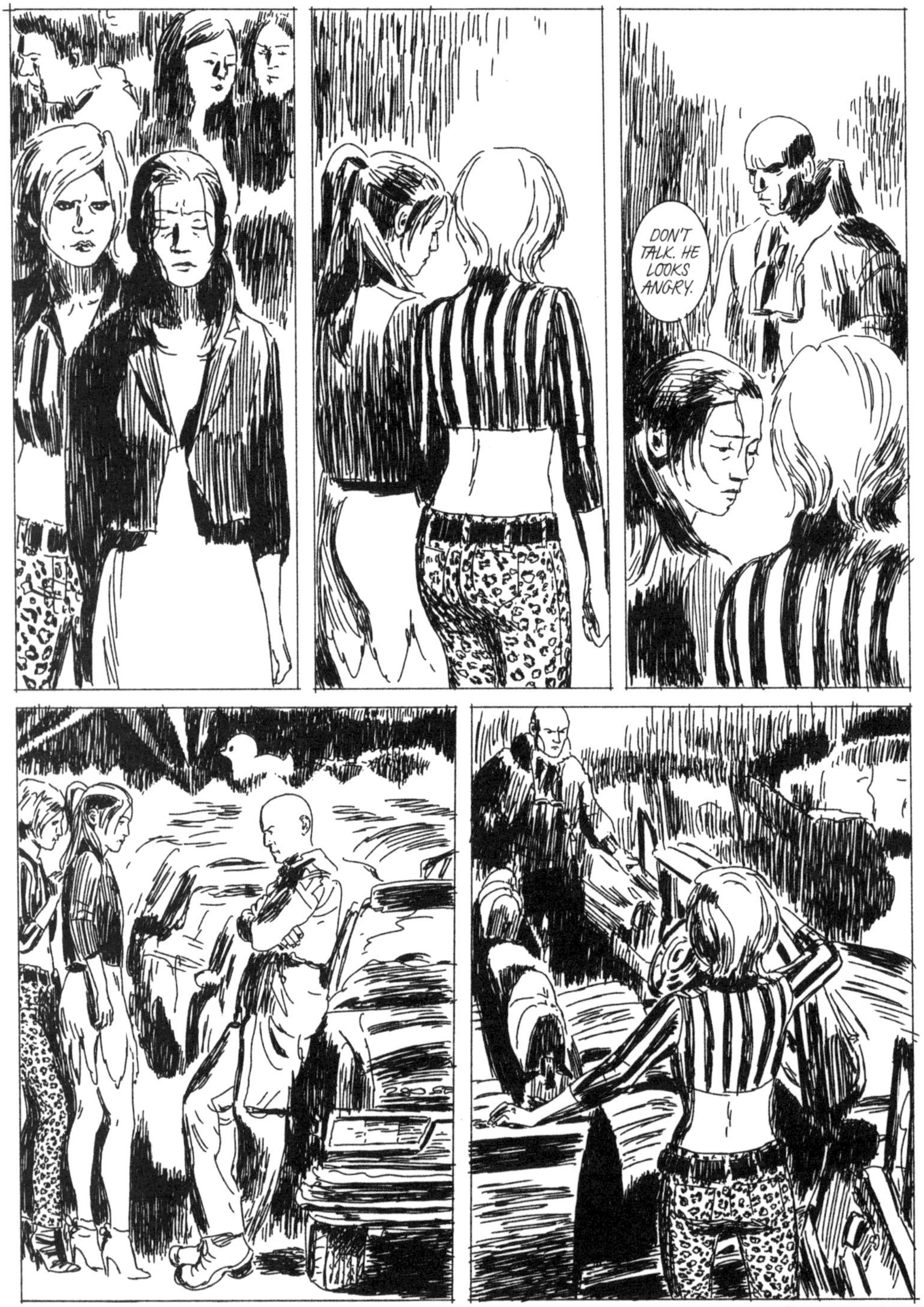
DON'T TALK. HE LOOKS ANGRY.

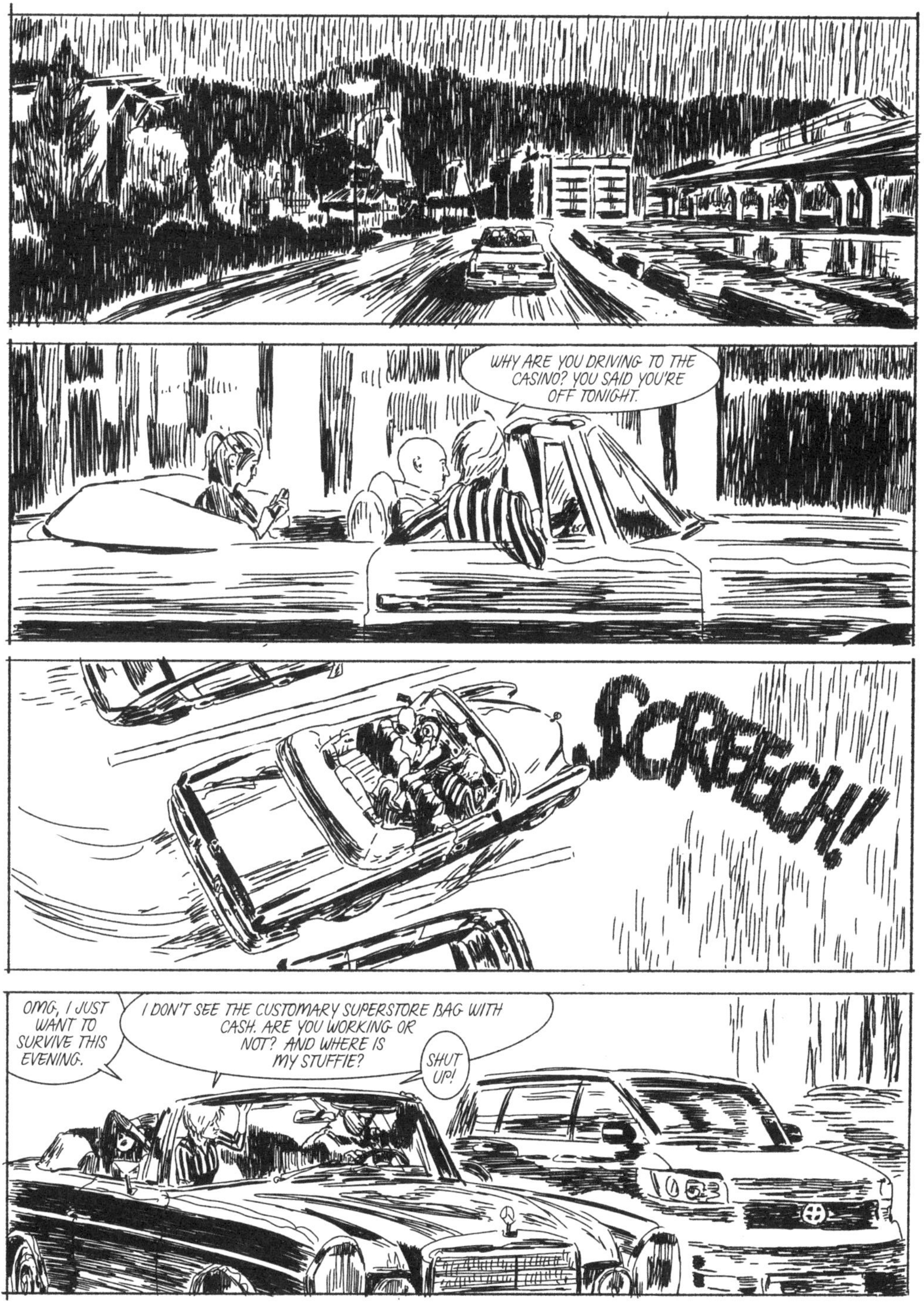

WHY ARE YOU DRIVING TO THE CASINO? YOU SAID YOU'RE OFF TONIGHT.
SCREECH!
OMG, I JUST WANT TO SURVIVE THIS EVENING.
I DON'T SEE THE CUSTOMARY SUPERSTORE BAG WITH CASH. ARE YOU WORKING OR NOT? AND WHERE IS MY STUFFIE?
SHUT UP!

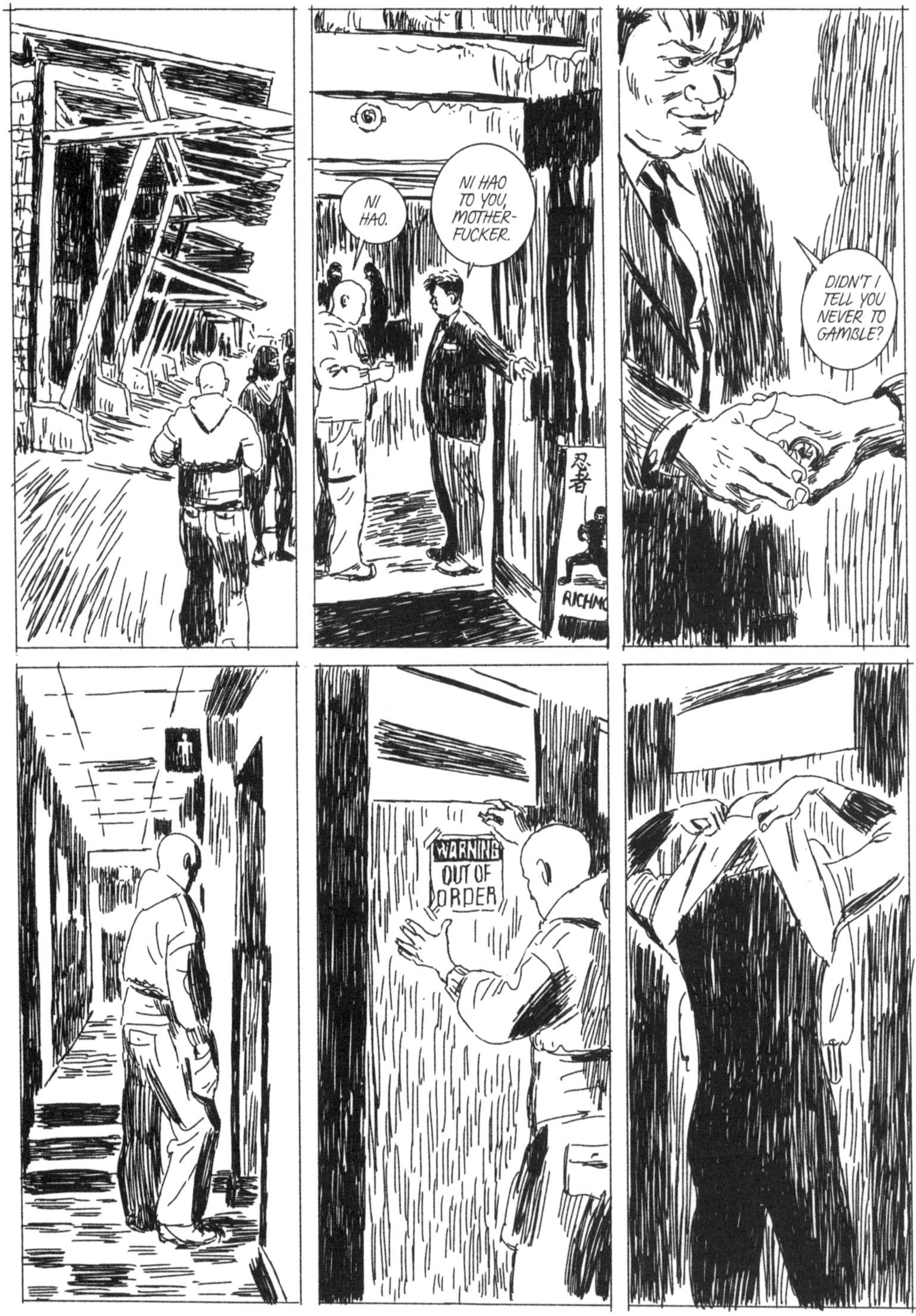
NI HAO.
NI HAO TO YOU, MOTHER-FUCKER.
忍者
RICHMO
DIDN'T I TELL YOU NEVER TO GAMBLE?
WARNING
OUT OF ORDER

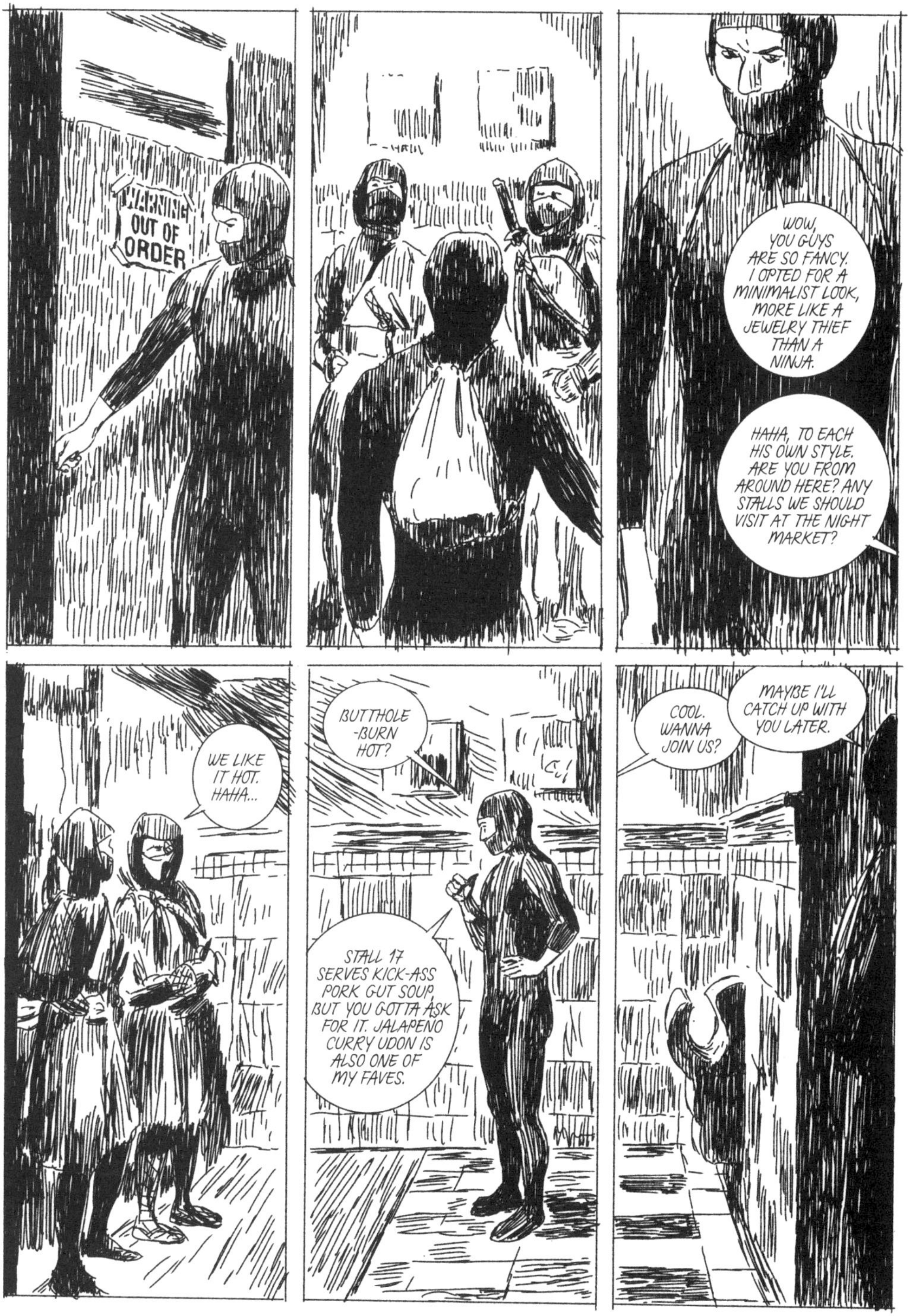
WARNING
OUT OF ORDER
WOW, YOU GUYS ARE SO FANCY. I OPTED FOR A MINIMALIST LOOK, MORE LIKE A JEWELRY THIEF THAN A NINJA.
HAHA, TO EACH HIS OWN STYLE. ARE YOU FROM AROUND HERE? ANY STALLS WE SHOULD VISIT AT THE NIGHT MARKET?
WE LIKE IT HOT. HAHA...
BUTTHOLE -BURN HOT?
STALL 17 SERVES KICK-ASS PORK GUT SOUP, BUT YOU GOTTA ASK FOR IT. JALAPENO CURRY UDON IS ALSO ONE OF MY FAVES.
COOL. WANNA JOIN US?
MAYBE I'LL CATCH UP WITH YOU LATER.

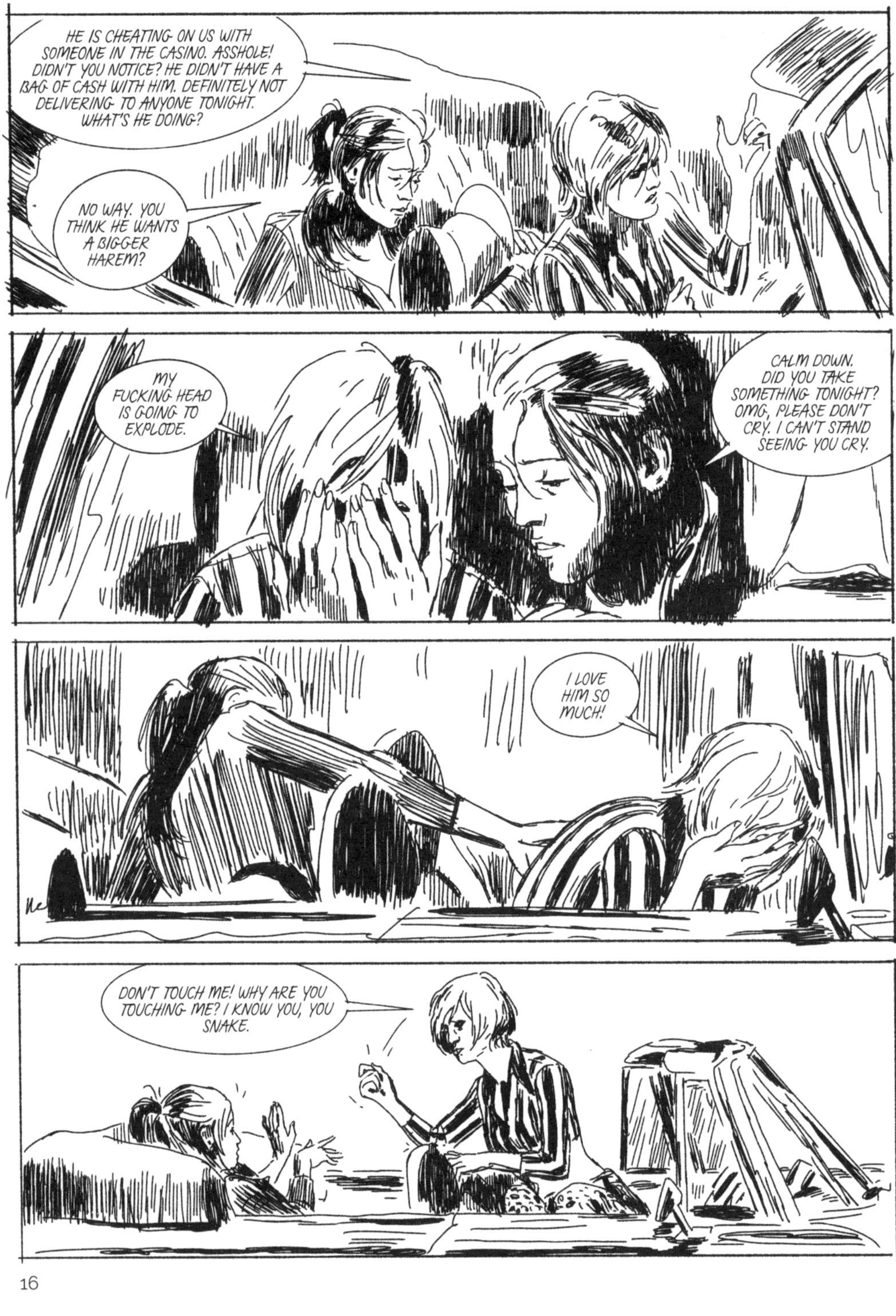
HE IS CHEATING ON US WITH SOMEONE IN THE CASINO. ASSHOLE! DIDN'T YOU NOTICE? HE DIDN'T HAVE A BAG OF CASH WITH HIM. DEFINITELY NOT DELIVERING TO ANYONE TONIGHT. WHAT'S HE DOING?
NO WAY. YOU THINK HE WANTS A BIGGER HAREM?
MY FUCKING HEAD IS GOING TO EXPLODE.
CALM DOWN. DID YOU TAKE SOMETHING TONIGHT? OMG, PLEASE DON'T CRY. I CAN'T STAND SEEING YOU CRY.
I LOVE HIM SO MUCH!
DON'T TOUCH ME! WHY ARE YOU TOUCHING ME? I KNOW YOU, YOU SNAKE.

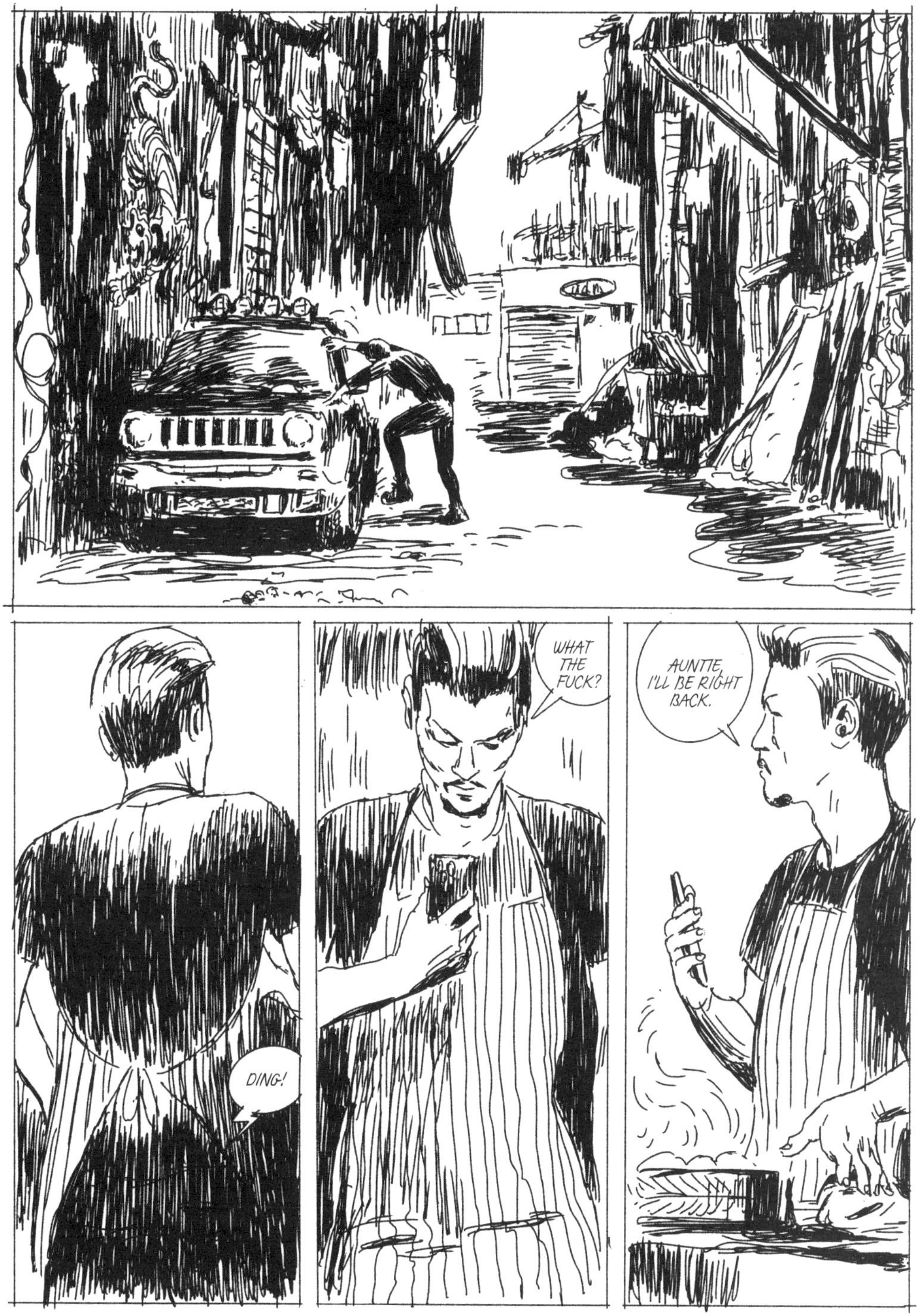
DING!
WHAT THE FUCK?
AUNTIE, I'LL BE RIGHT BACK.

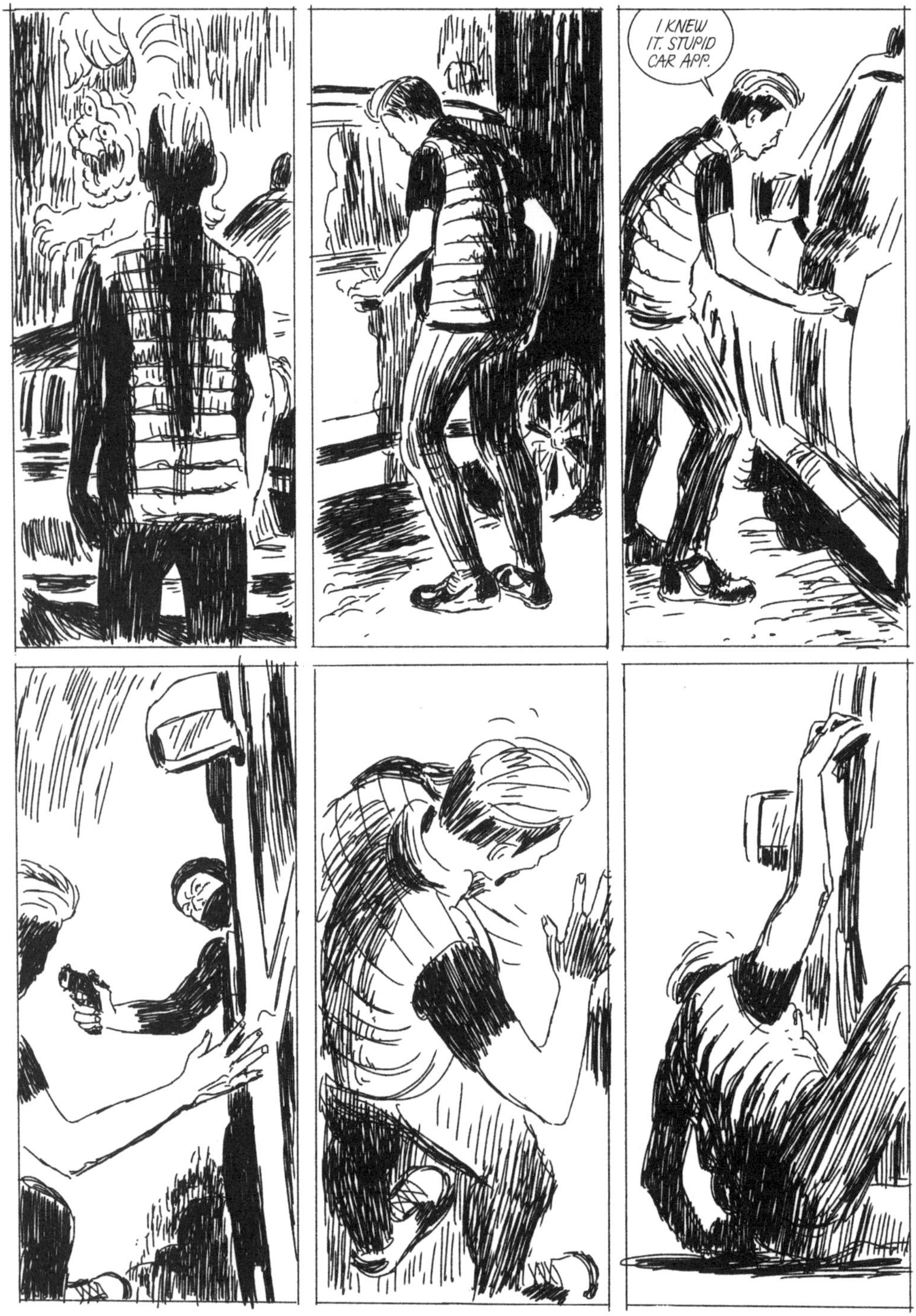
I KNEW IT. STUPID CAR APP.

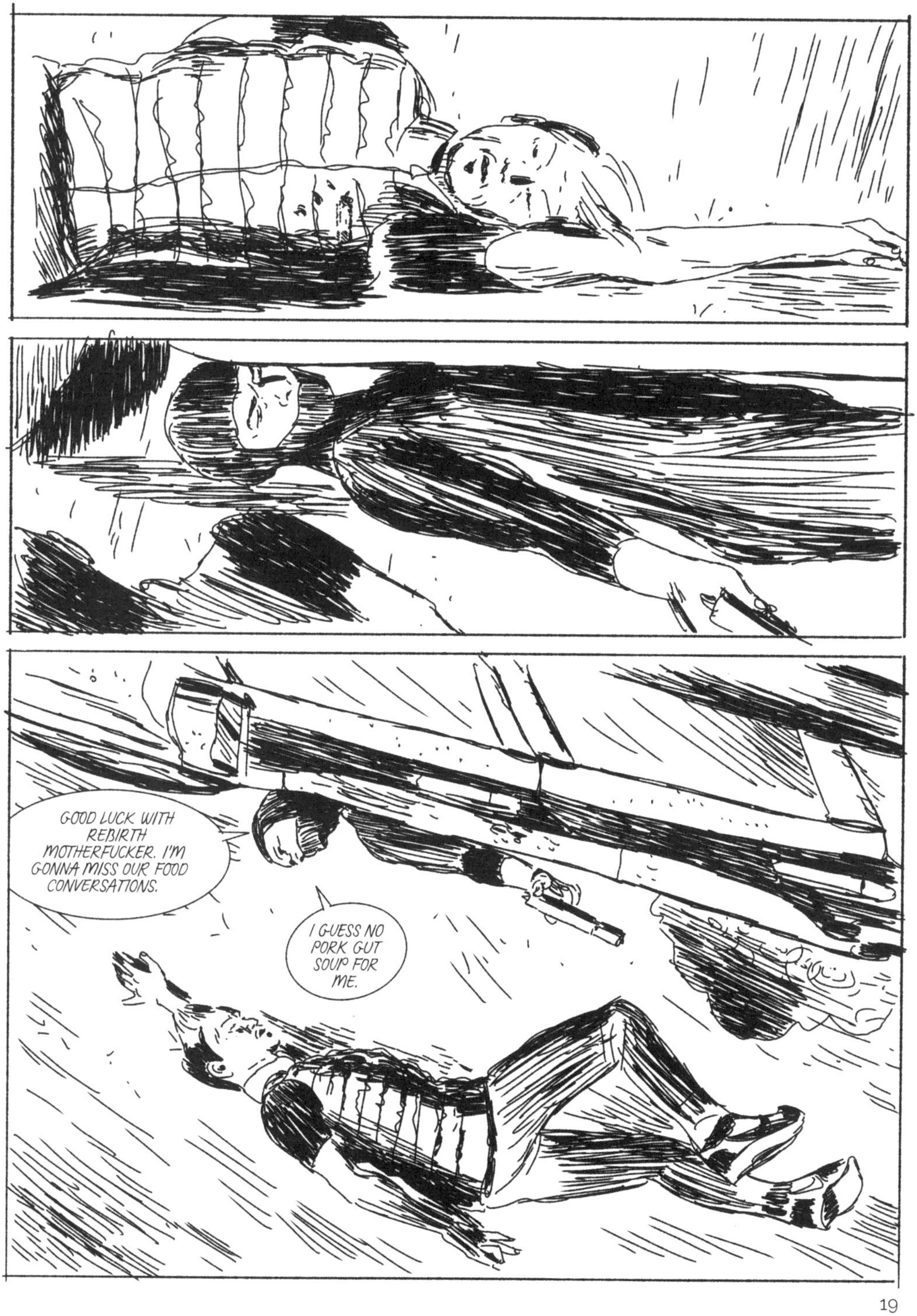
GOOD LUCK WITH REBIRTH MOTHERFUCKER. I'M GONNA MISS OUR FOOD CONVERSATIONS.
I GUESS NO PORK GUT SOUP FOR ME.

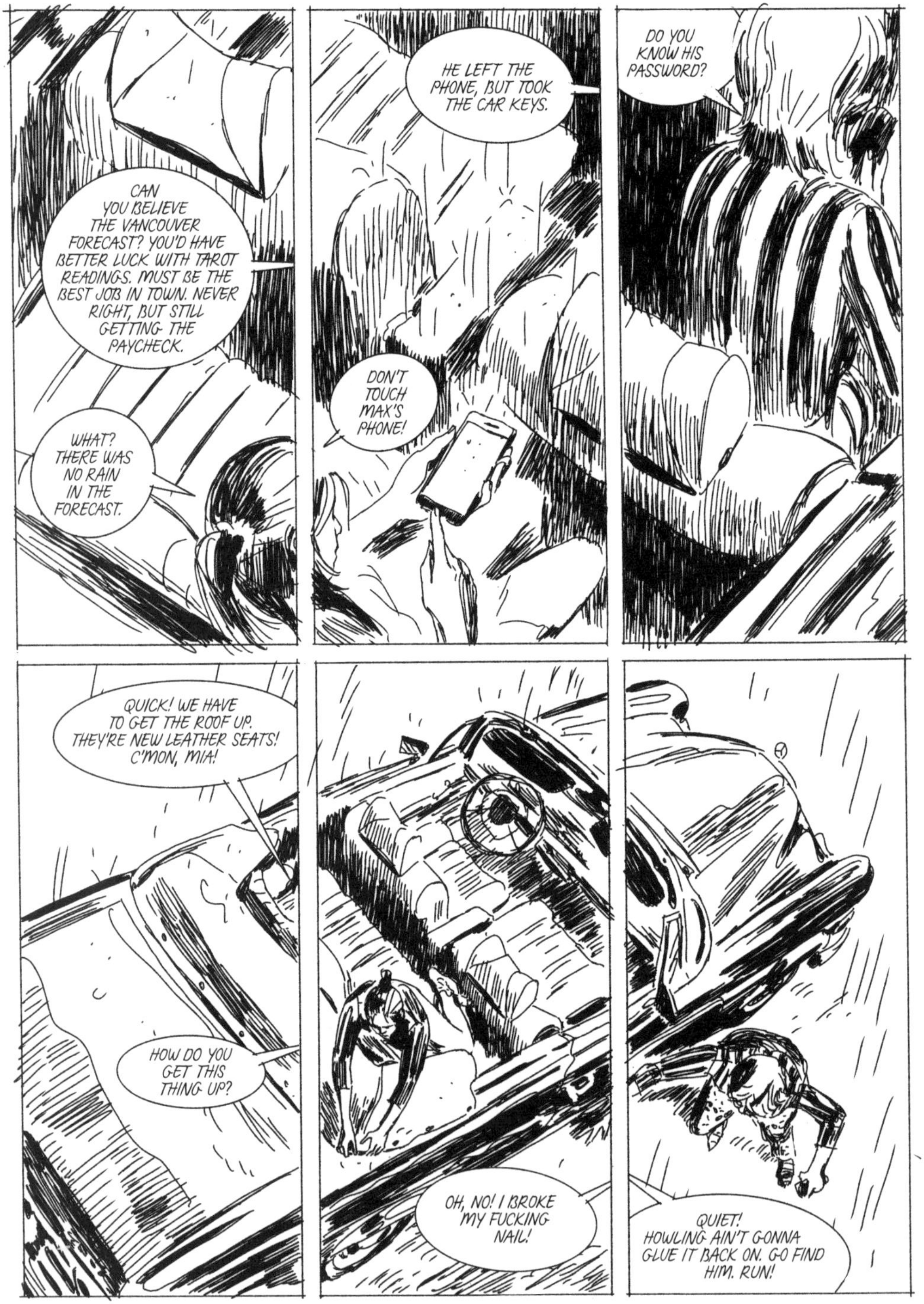
CAN YOU BELIEVE THE VANCOUVER FORECAST? YOU'D HAVE BETTER LUCK WITH TAROT READINGS. MUST BE THE BEST JOB IN TOWN. NEVER RIGHT, BUT STILL GETTING THE PAYCHECK.
WHAT? THERE WAS NO RAIN IN THE FORECAST.
HE LEFT THE PHONE, BUT TOOK THE CAR KEYS.
DON'T TOUCH MAX'S PHONE!
DO YOU KNOW HIS PASSWORD?
QUICK! WE HAVE TO GET THE ROOF UP. THEY'RE NEW LEATHER SEATS! C'MON, MIA!
HOW DO YOU GET THIS THING UP?
OH, NO! I BROKE MY FUCKING NAIL!
QUIET! HOWLING AIN'T GONNA GLUE IT BACK ON. GO FIND HIM. RUN!

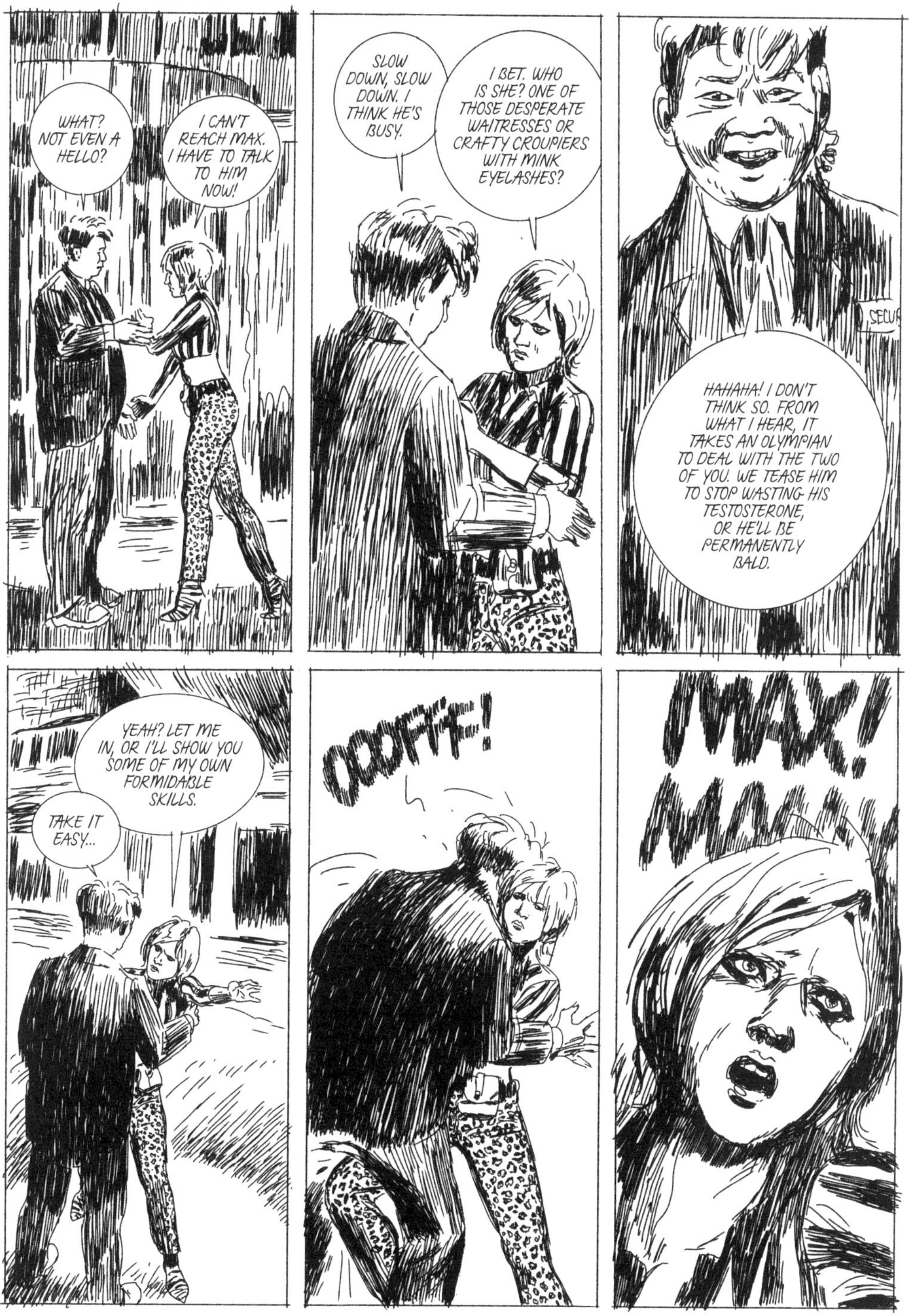
WHAT? NOT EVEN A HELLO?
I CAN'T REACH MAX. I HAVE TO TALK TO HIM NOW!
SLOW DOWN, SLOW DOWN. I THINK HE'S BUSY.
I BET. WHO IS SHE? ONE OF THOSE DESPERATE WAITRESSES OR CRAFTY CROUPIERS WITH MINK EYELASHES?
HAHAHA! I DON'T THINK SO. FROM WHAT I HEAR, IT TAKES AN OLYMPIAN TO DEAL WITH THE TWO OF YOU. WE TEASE HIM TO STOP WASTING HIS TESTOSTERONE, OR HE'LL BE PERMANENTLY BALD.
YEAH? LET ME IN, OR I'LL SHOW YOU SOME OF MY OWN FORMIDABLE SKILLS.
TAKE IT EASY...
OOOFFF!
MAX!

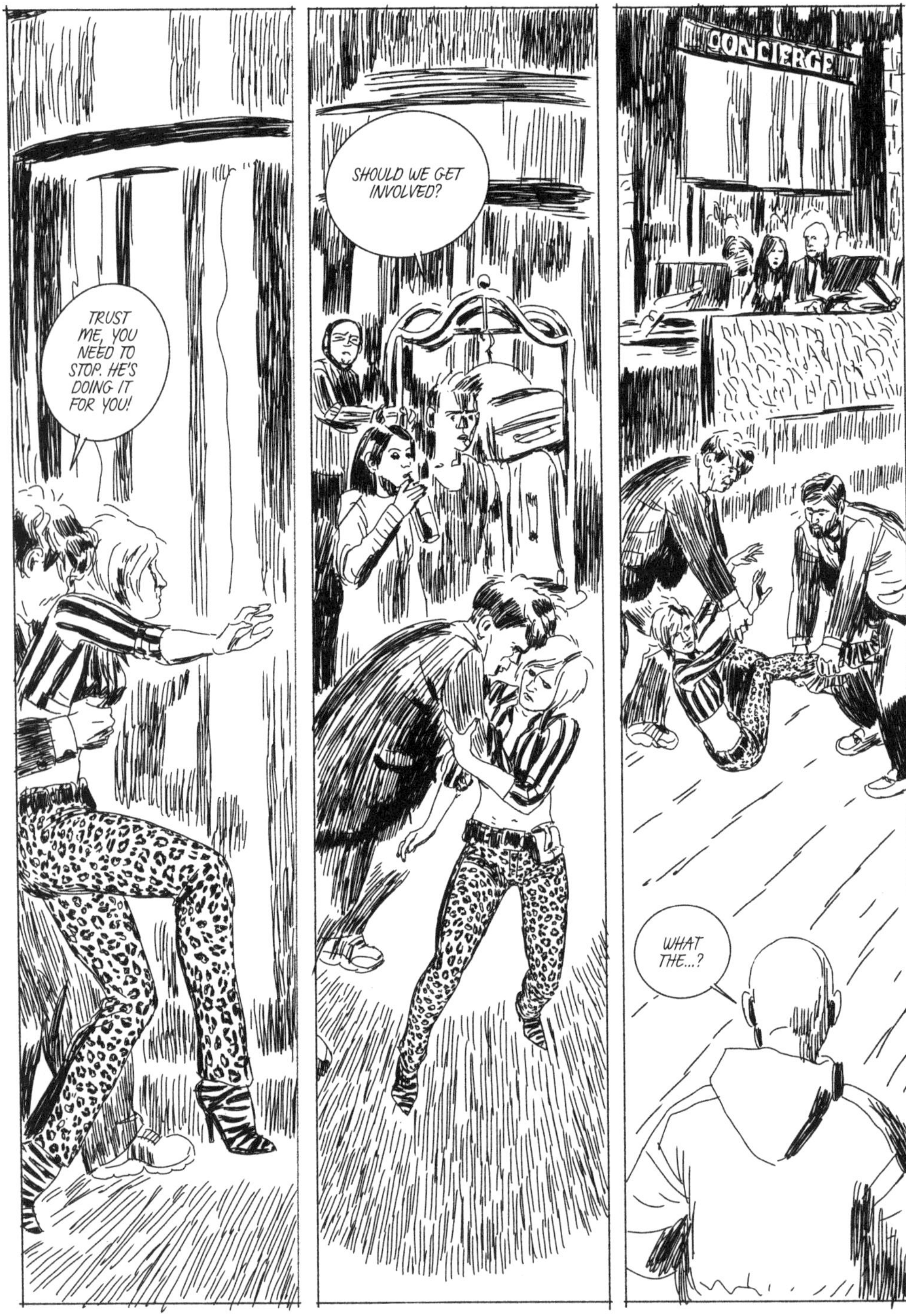
TRUST ME, YOU NEED TO STOP. HE'S DOING IT FOR YOU!
SHOULD WE GET INVOLVED?
CONCIERGE
WHAT THE...?

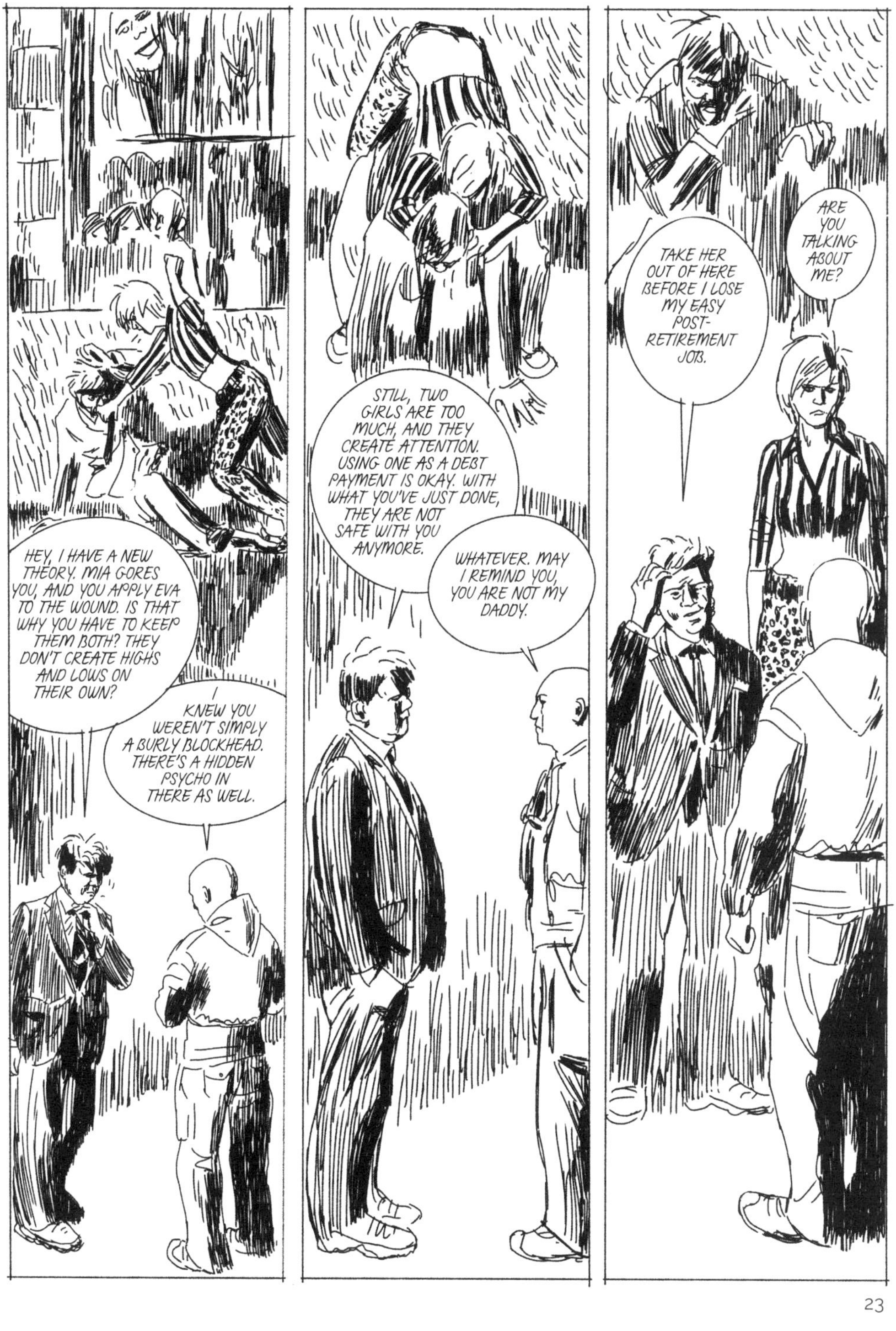
HEY, I HAVE A NEW THEORY. MIA GORES YOU, AND YOU APPLY EVA TO THE WOUND. IS THAT WHY YOU HAVE TO KEEP THEM BOTH? THEY DON'T CREATE HIGHS AND LOWS ON THEIR OWN?
I KNEW YOU WEREN'T SIMPLY A BURLY BLOCKHEAD. THERE'S A HIDDEN PSYCHO IN THERE AS WELL.
STILL, TWO GIRLS ARE TOO MUCH, AND THEY CREATE ATTENTION. USING ONE AS A DEBT PAYMENT IS OKAY. WITH WHAT YOU'VE JUST DONE, THEY ARE NOT SAFE WITH YOU ANYMORE.
WHATEVER. MAY I REMIND YOU, YOU ARE NOT MY DADDY.
TAKE HER OUT OF HERE BEFORE I LOSE MY EASY POST-RETIREMENT JOB.
ARE YOU TALKING ABOUT ME?

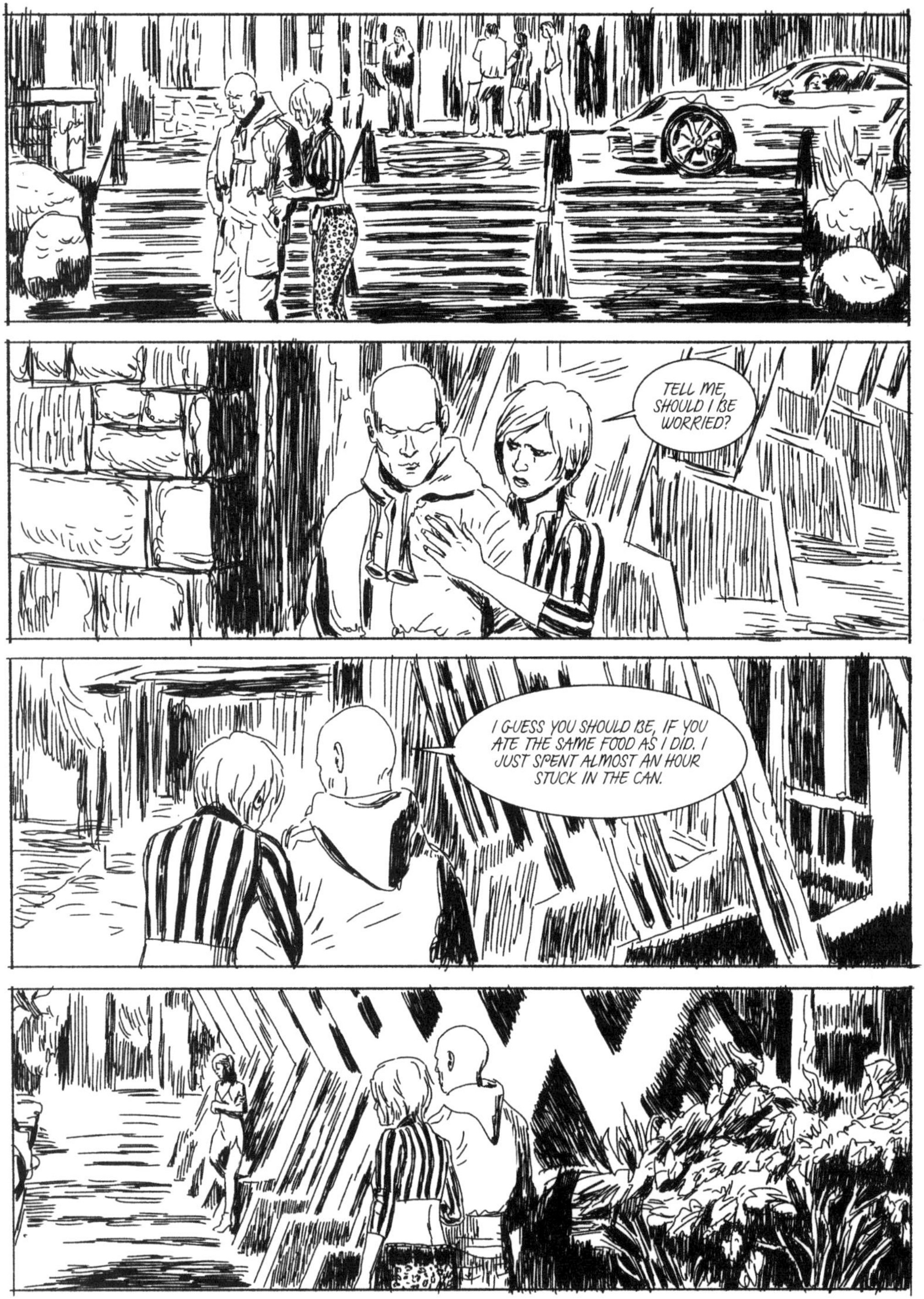
TELL ME, SHOULD I BE WORRIED?
I GUESS YOU SHOULD BE, IF YOU ATE THE SAME FOOD AS I DID. I JUST SPENT ALMOST AN HOUR STUCK IN THE CAN.

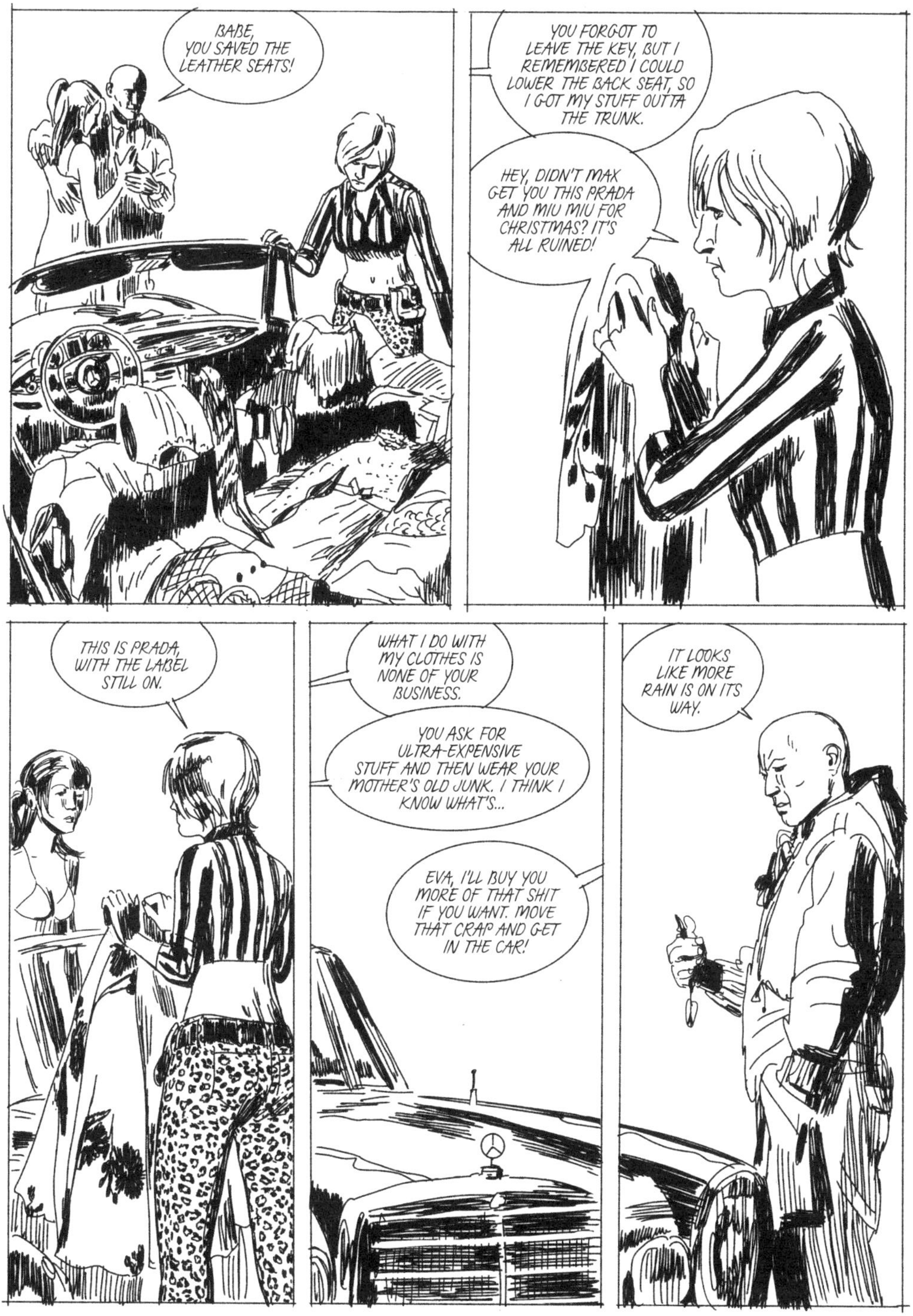
BABE, YOU SAVED THE LEATHER SEATS!
YOU FORGOT TO LEAVE THE KEY, BUT I REMEMBERED I COULD LOWER THE BACK SEAT, SO I GOT MY STUFF OUTTA THE TRUNK.
HEY, DIDN'T MAX GET YOU THIS PRADA AND MIU MIU FOR CHRISTMAS? IT'S ALL RUINED!
THIS IS PRADA, WITH THE LABEL STILL ON.
WHAT I DO WITH MY CLOTHES IS NONE OF YOUR BUSINESS.
YOU ASK FOR ULTRA-EXPENSIVE STUFF AND THEN WEAR YOUR MOTHER'S OLD JUNK. I THINK I KNOW WHAT'S...
EVA, I'LL BUY YOU MORE OF THAT SHIT IF YOU WANT. MOVE THAT CRAP AND GET IN THE CAR!
IT LOOKS LIKE MORE RAIN IS ON ITS WAY.

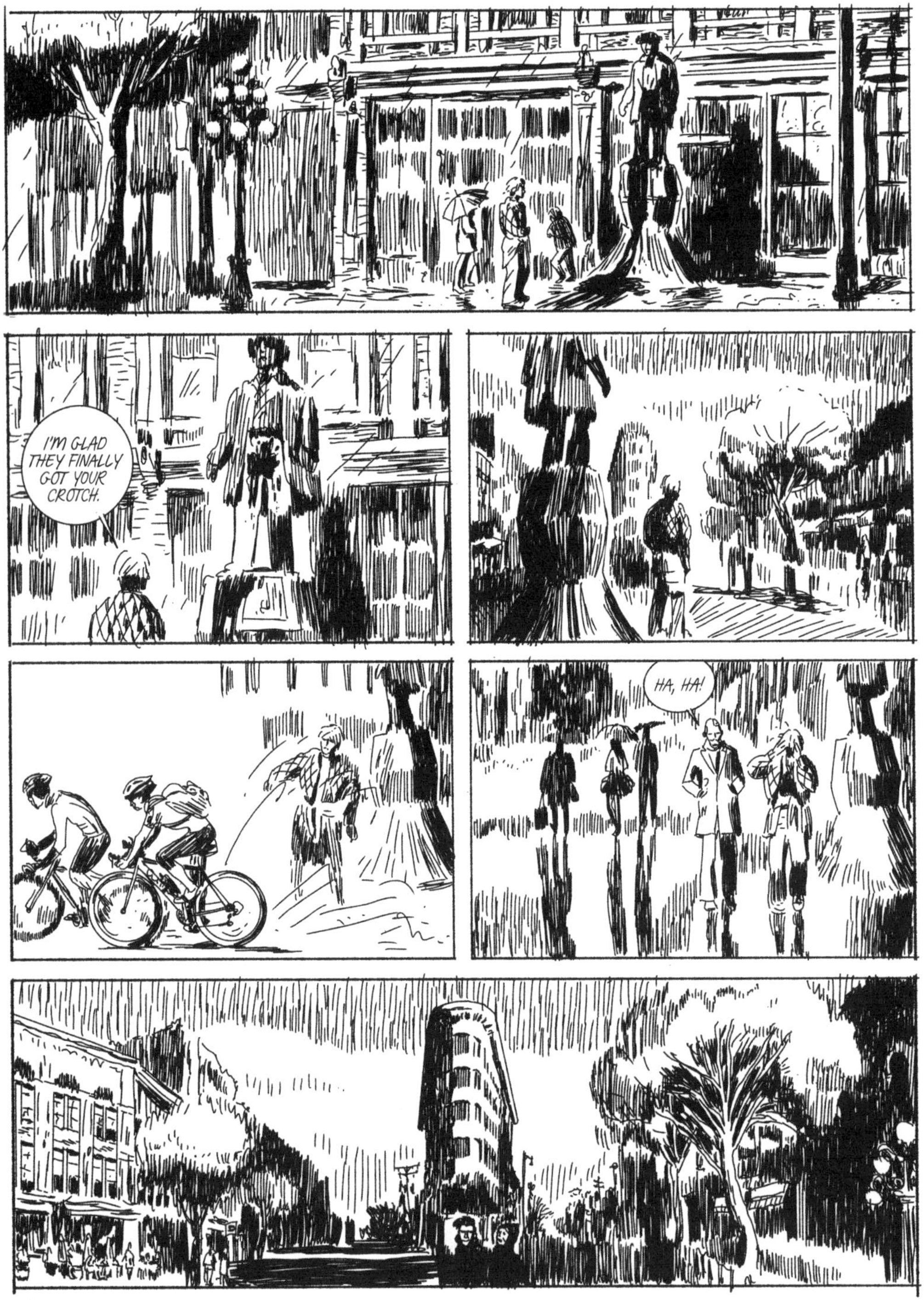
I'M GLAD THEY FINALLY GOT YOUR CROTCH.
HA, HA!

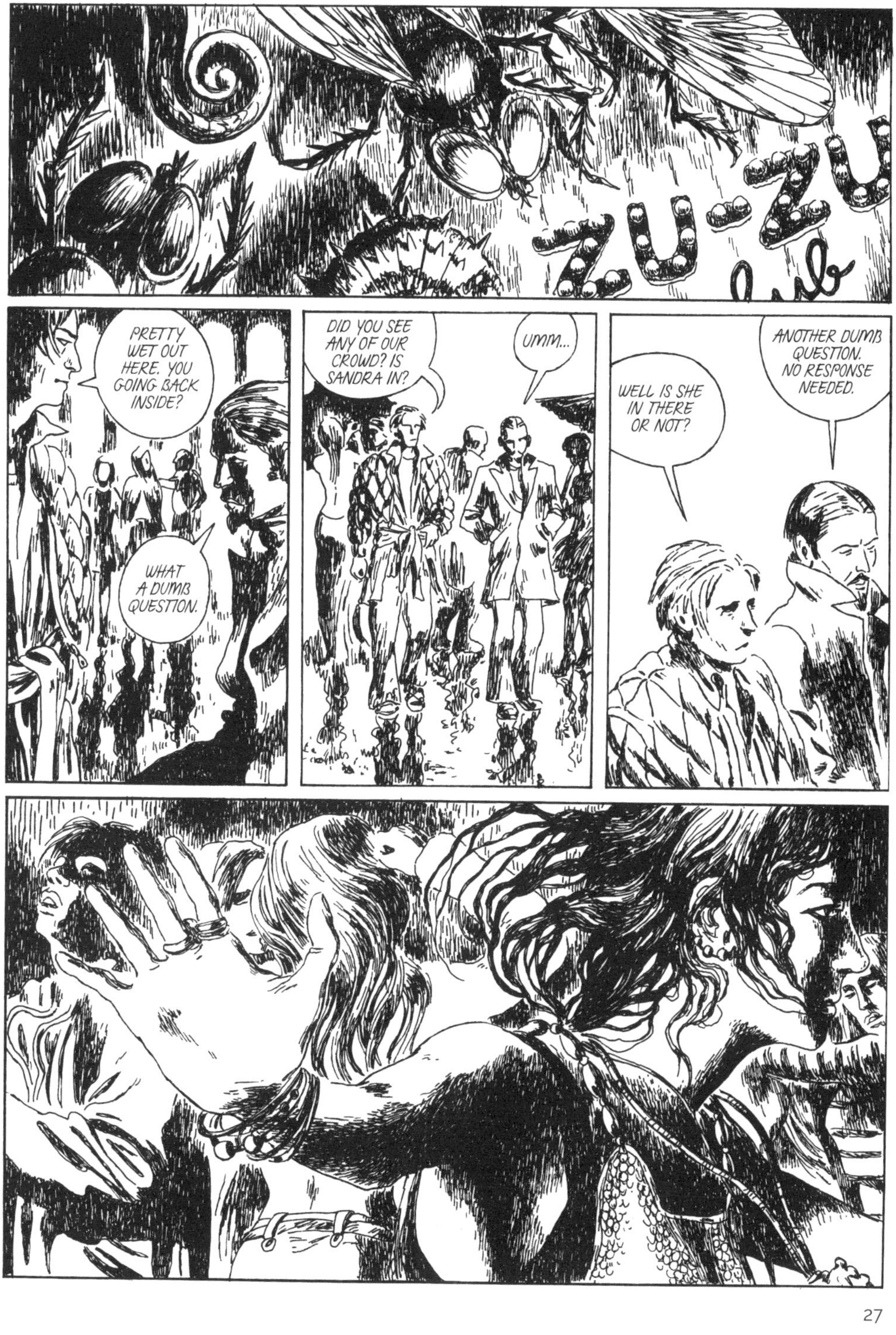
ZU-ZU
PRETTY WET OUT HERE. YOU GOING BACK INSIDE?
WHAT A DUMB QUESTION.
DID YOU SEE ANY OF OUR CROWD? IS SANDRA IN?
UMM...
WELL IS SHE IN THERE OR NOT?
ANOTHER DUMB QUESTION. NO RESPONSE NEEDED.

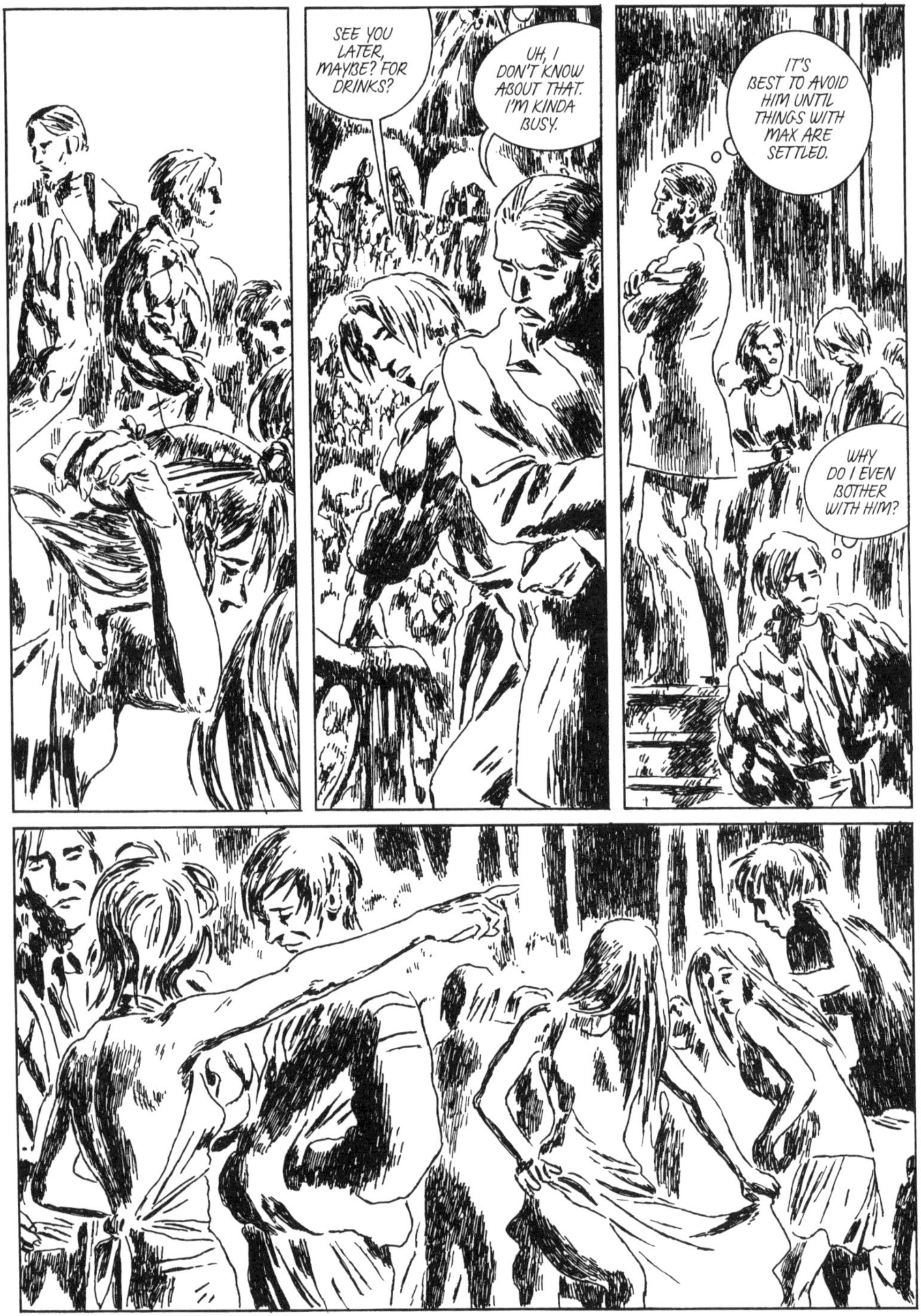
SEE YOU LATER, MAYBE? FOR DRINKS?
UH, I DON'T KNOW ABOUT THAT. I'M KINDA BUSY.
IT'S BEST TO AVOID HIM UNTIL THINGS WITH MAX ARE SETTLED.
WHY DO I EVEN BOTHER WITH HIM?

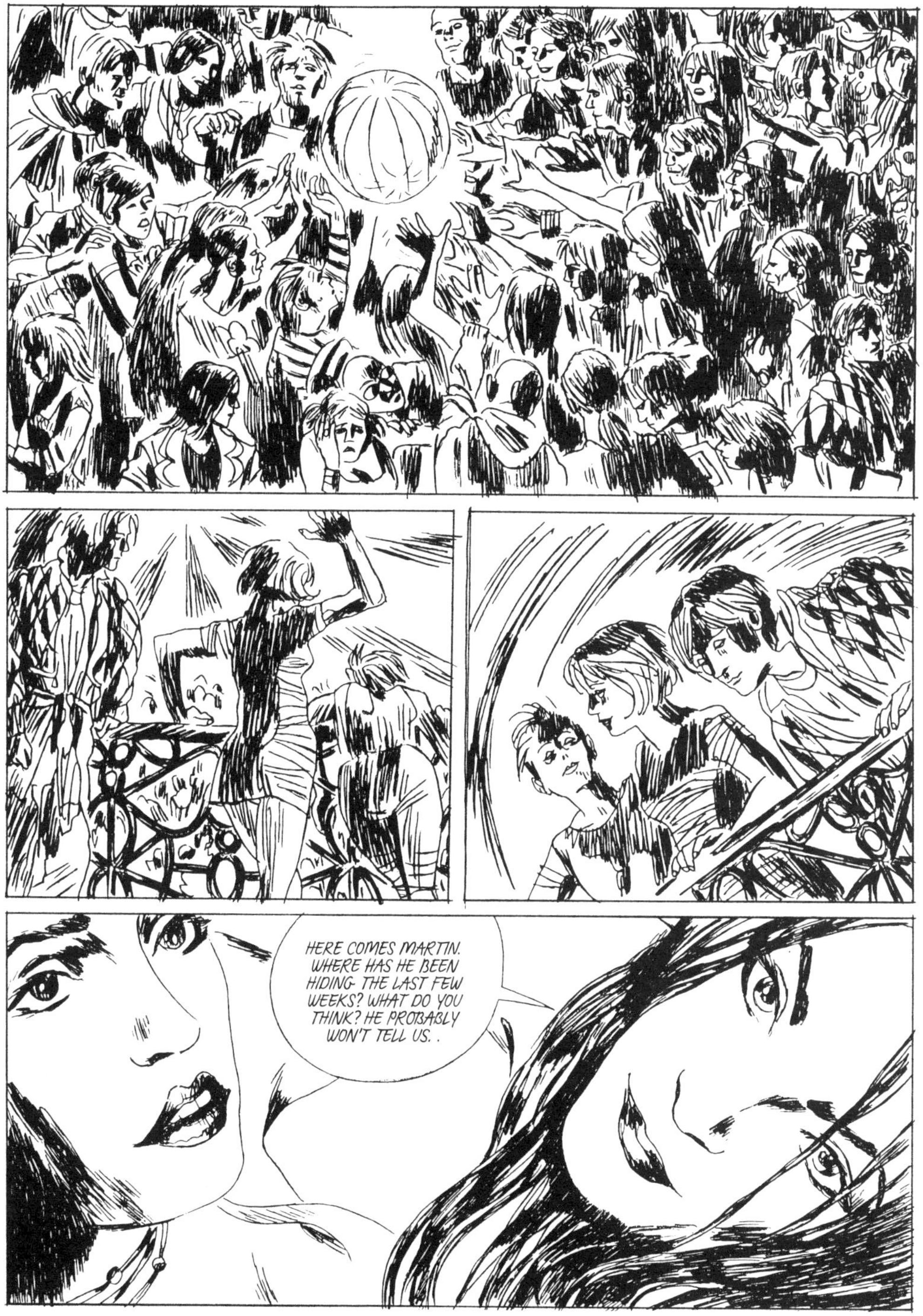
HERE COMES MARTIN. WHERE HAS HE BEEN HIDING THE LAST FEW WEEKS? WHAT DO YOU THINK? HE PROBABLY WON'T TELL US. .

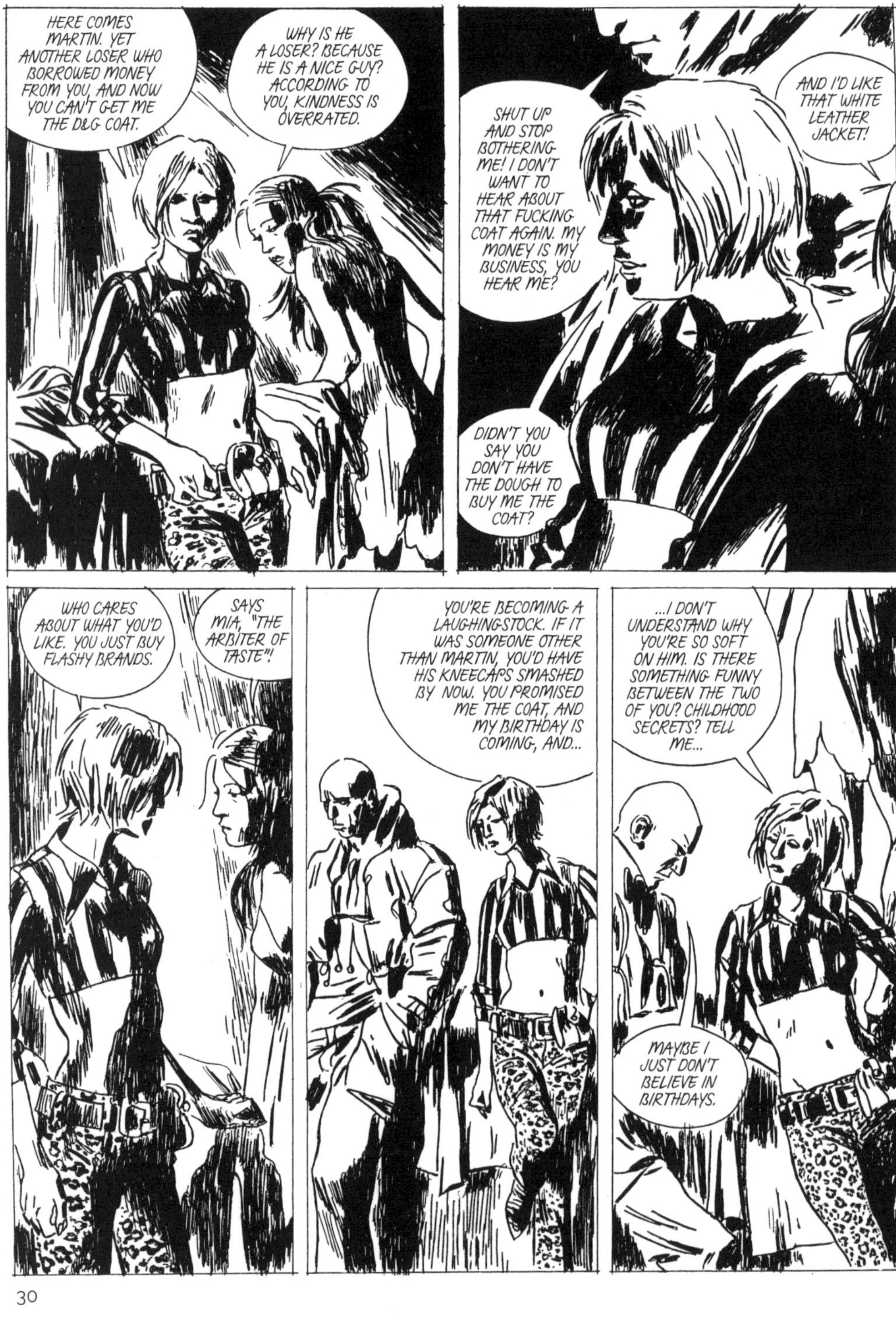
HERE COMES MARTIN. YET ANOTHER LOSER WHO BORROWED MONEY FROM YOU, AND NOW YOU CAN'T GET ME THE D&G COAT.
WHY IS HE A LOSER? BECAUSE HE IS A NICE GUY? ACCORDING TO YOU, KINDNESS IS OVERRATED.
SHUT UP AND STOP BOTHERING ME! I DON'T WANT TO HEAR ABOUT THAT FUCKING COAT AGAIN. MY MONEY IS MY BUSINESS, YOU HEAR ME?
AND I'D LIKE THAT WHITE LEATHER JACKET!
DIDN'T YOU SAY YOU DON'T HAVE THE DOUGH TO BUY ME THE COAT?
WHO CARES ABOUT WHAT YOU'D LIKE. YOU JUST BUY FLASHY BRANDS.
SAYS MIA, "THE ARBITER OF TASTE"!
YOU'RE BECOMING A LAUGHINGSTOCK. IF IT WAS SOMEONE OTHER THAN MARTIN, YOU'D HAVE HIS KNEECAPS SMASHED BY NOW. YOU PROMISED ME THE COAT, AND MY BIRTHDAY IS COMING, AND...
...I DON'T UNDERSTAND WHY YOU'RE SO SOFT ON HIM. IS THERE SOMETHING FUNNY BETWEEN THE TWO OF YOU? CHILDHOOD SECRETS? TELL ME...
MAYBE I JUST DON'T BELIEVE IN BIRTHDAYS.

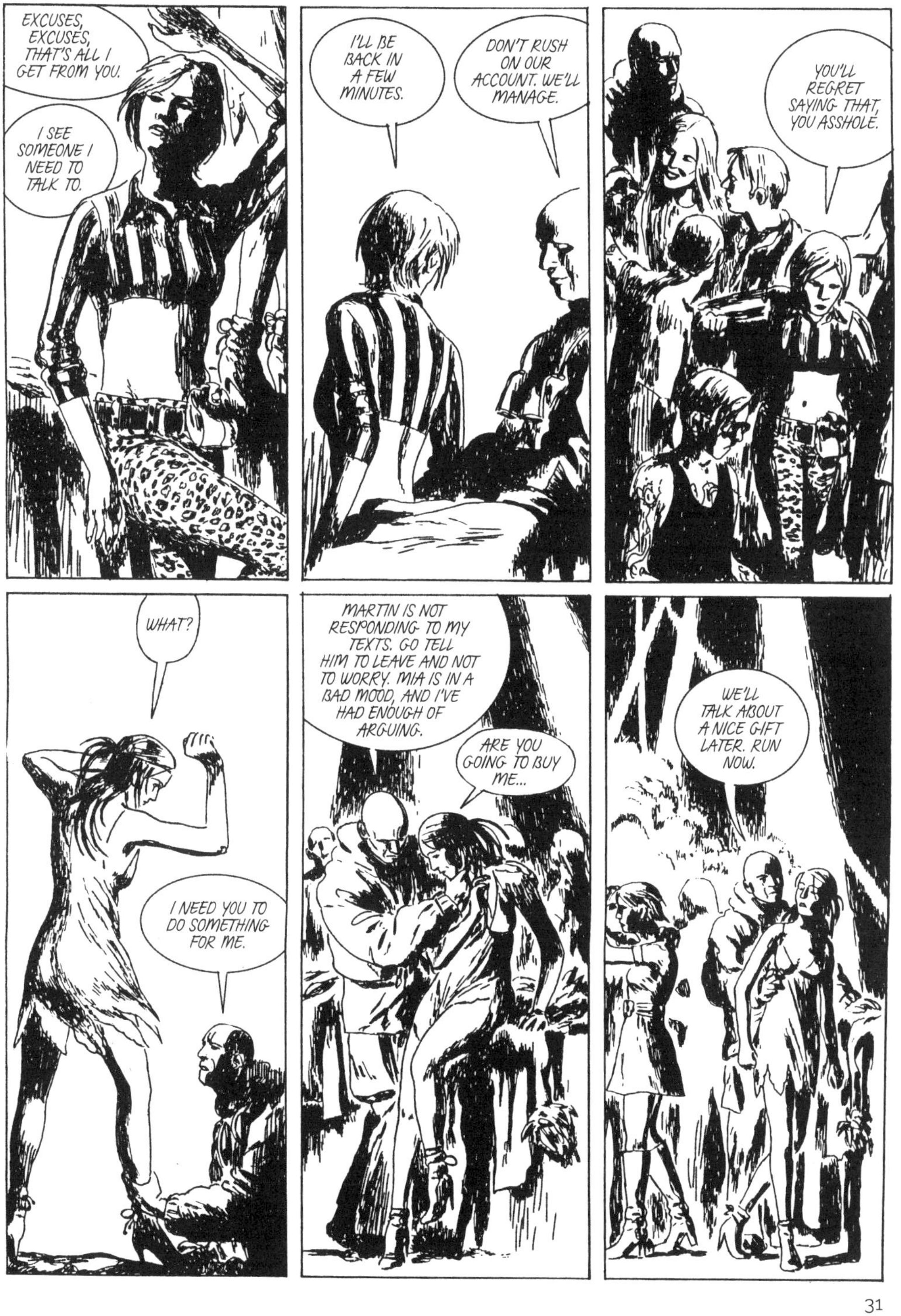

EXCUSES, EXCUSES, THAT'S ALL I GET FROM YOU.
I SEE SOMEONE I NEED TO TALK TO.
I'LL BE BACK IN A FEW MINUTES.
DON'T RUSH ON OUR ACCOUNT. WE'LL MANAGE.
YOU'LL REGRET SAYING THAT, YOU ASSHOLE.
WHAT?
I NEED YOU TO DO SOMETHING FOR ME.
MARTIN IS NOT RESPONDING TO MY TEXTS. GO TELL HIM TO LEAVE AND NOT TO WORRY. MIA IS IN A BAD MOOD, AND I'VE HAD ENOUGH OF ARGUING.
ARE YOU GOING TO BUY ME...
WE'LL TALK ABOUT A NICE GIFT LATER. RUN NOW.

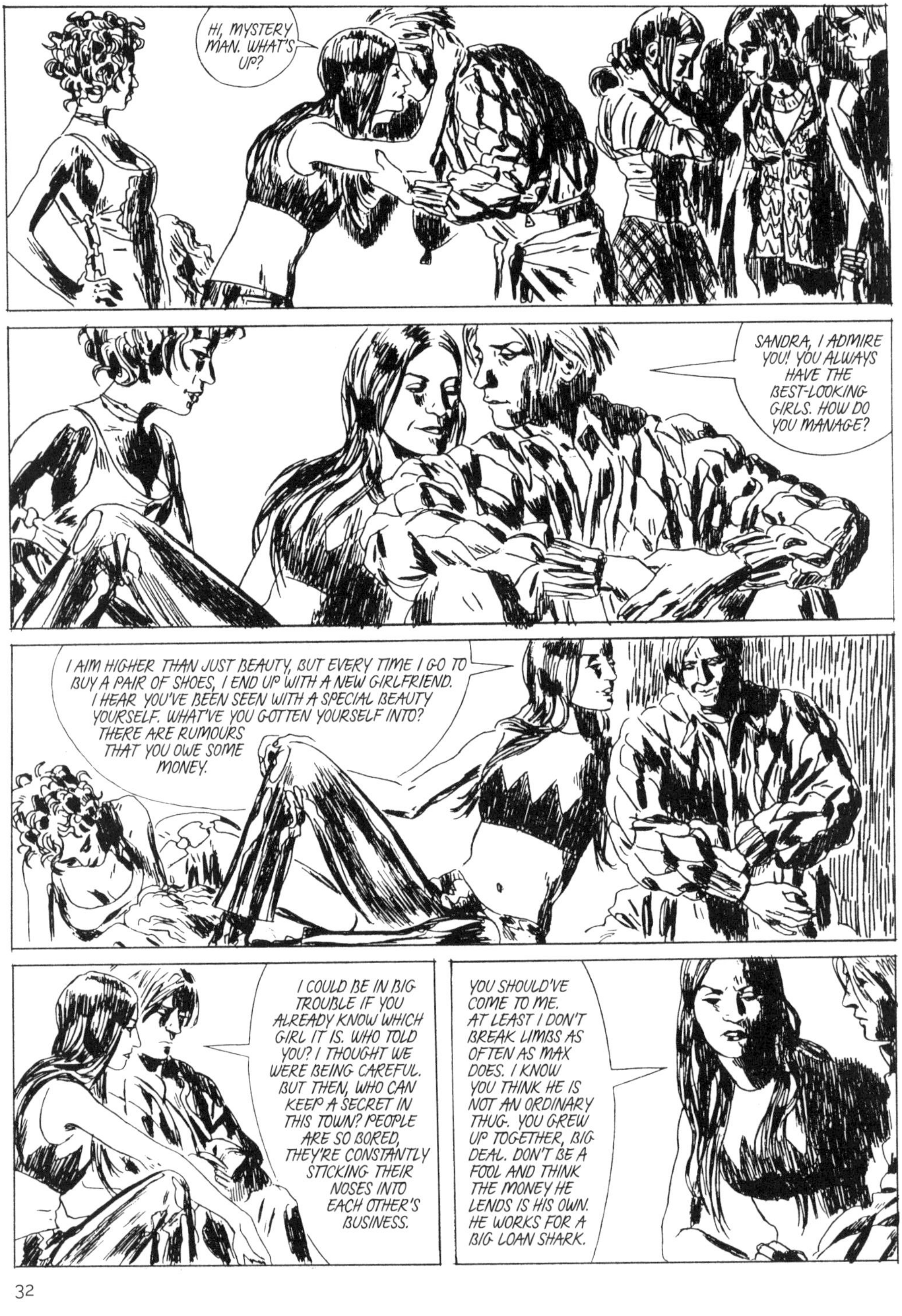
HI, MYSTERY MAN. WHAT'S UP?
SANDRA, I ADMIRE YOU! YOU ALWAYS HAVE THE BEST-LOOKING GIRLS. HOW DO YOU MANAGE?
I AIM HIGHER THAN JUST BEAUTY, BUT EVERY TIME I GO TO BUY A PAIR OF SHOES, I END UP WITH A NEW GIRLFRIEND. I HEAR YOU'VE BEEN SEEN WITH A SPECIAL BEAUTY YOURSELF. WHAT'VE YOU GOTTEN YOURSELF INTO? THERE ARE RUMOURS THAT YOU OWE SOME MONEY.
I COULD BE IN BIG TROUBLE IF YOU ALREADY KNOW WHICH GIRL IT IS. WHO TOLD YOU? I THOUGHT WE WERE BEING CAREFUL. BUT THEN, WHO CAN KEEP A SECRET IN THIS TOWN? PEOPLE ARE SO BORED, THEY'RE CONSTANTLY STICKING THEIR NOSES INTO EACH OTHER'S BUSINESS.
YOU SHOULD'VE COME TO ME. AT LEAST I DON'T BREAK LIMBS AS OFTEN AS MAX DOES. I KNOW YOU THINK HE IS NOT AN ORDINARY THUG. YOU GREW UP TOGETHER, BIG DEAL. DON'T BE A FOOL AND THINK THE MONEY HE LENDS IS HIS OWN. HE WORKS FOR A BIG LOAN SHARK.

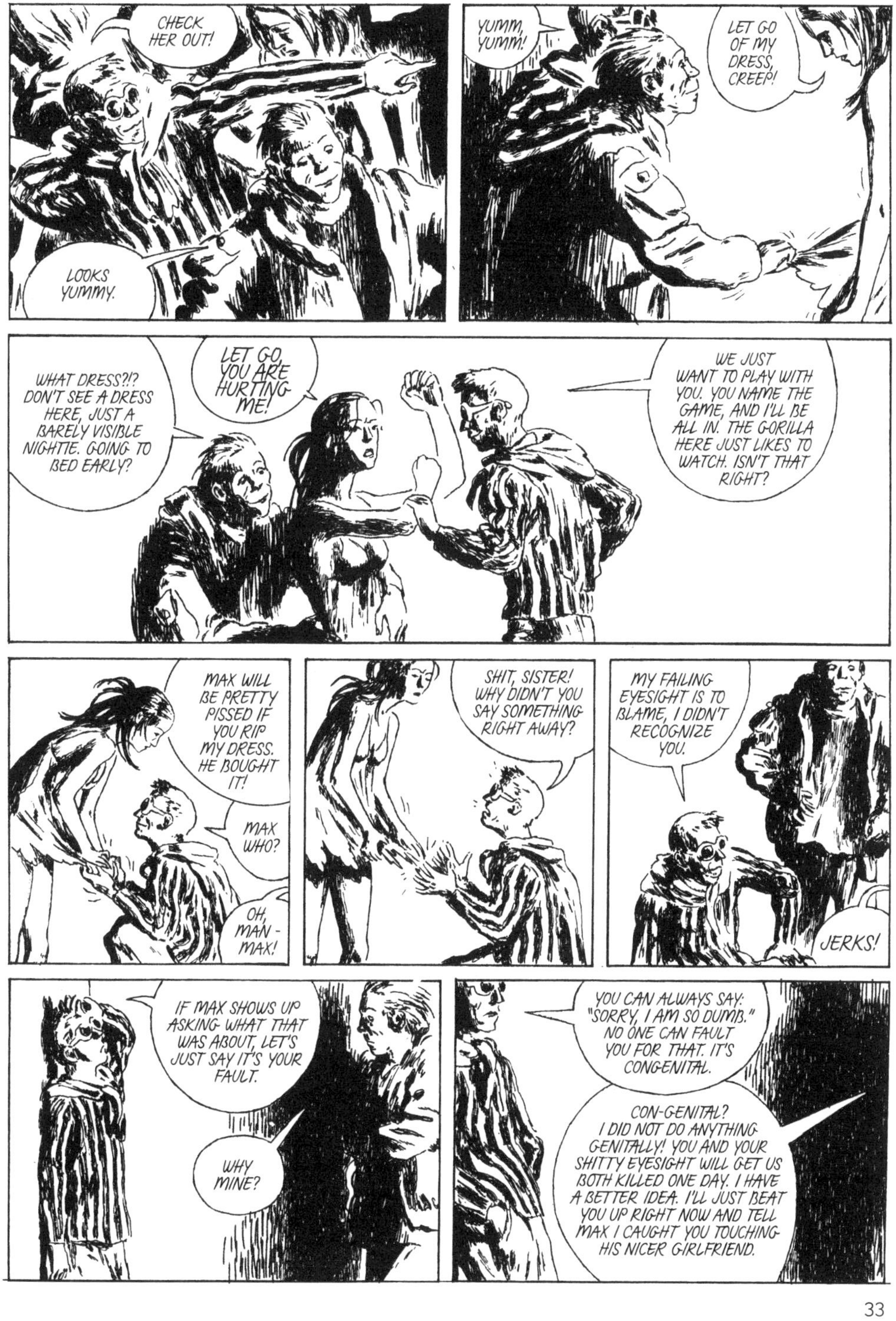

CHECK HER OUT!
LOOKS YUMMY.
YUMM, YUMM!
LET GO OF MY DRESS, CREEP!
WHAT DRESS?!? DON'T SEE A DRESS HERE, JUST A BARELY VISIBLE NIGHTIE. GOING TO BED EARLY?
LET GO, YOU ARE HURTING ME!
WE JUST WANT TO PLAY WITH YOU. YOU NAME THE GAME, AND I'LL BE ALL IN. THE GORILLA HERE JUST LIKES TO WATCH. ISN'T THAT RIGHT?
MAX WILL BE PRETTY PISSED IF YOU RIP MY DRESS. HE BOUGHT IT!
MAX WHO?
OH, MAN - MAX!
SHIT, SISTER! WHY DIDN'T YOU SAY SOMETHING RIGHT AWAY?
MY FAILING EYESIGHT IS TO BLAME, I DIDN'T RECOGNIZE YOU.
JERKS!
IF MAX SHOWS UP ASKING WHAT THAT WAS ABOUT, LET'S JUST SAY IT'S YOUR FAULT.
WHY MINE?
YOU CAN ALWAYS SAY: "SORRY, I AM SO DUMB." NO ONE CAN FAULT YOU FOR THAT. IT'S CONGENITAL.
CON-GENITAL? I DID NOT DO ANYTHING GENITALLY! YOU AND YOUR SHITTY EYESIGHT WILL GET US BOTH KILLED ONE DAY. I HAVE A BETTER IDEA. I'LL JUST BEAT YOU UP RIGHT NOW AND TELL MAX I CAUGHT YOU TOUCHING HIS NICER GIRLFRIEND.

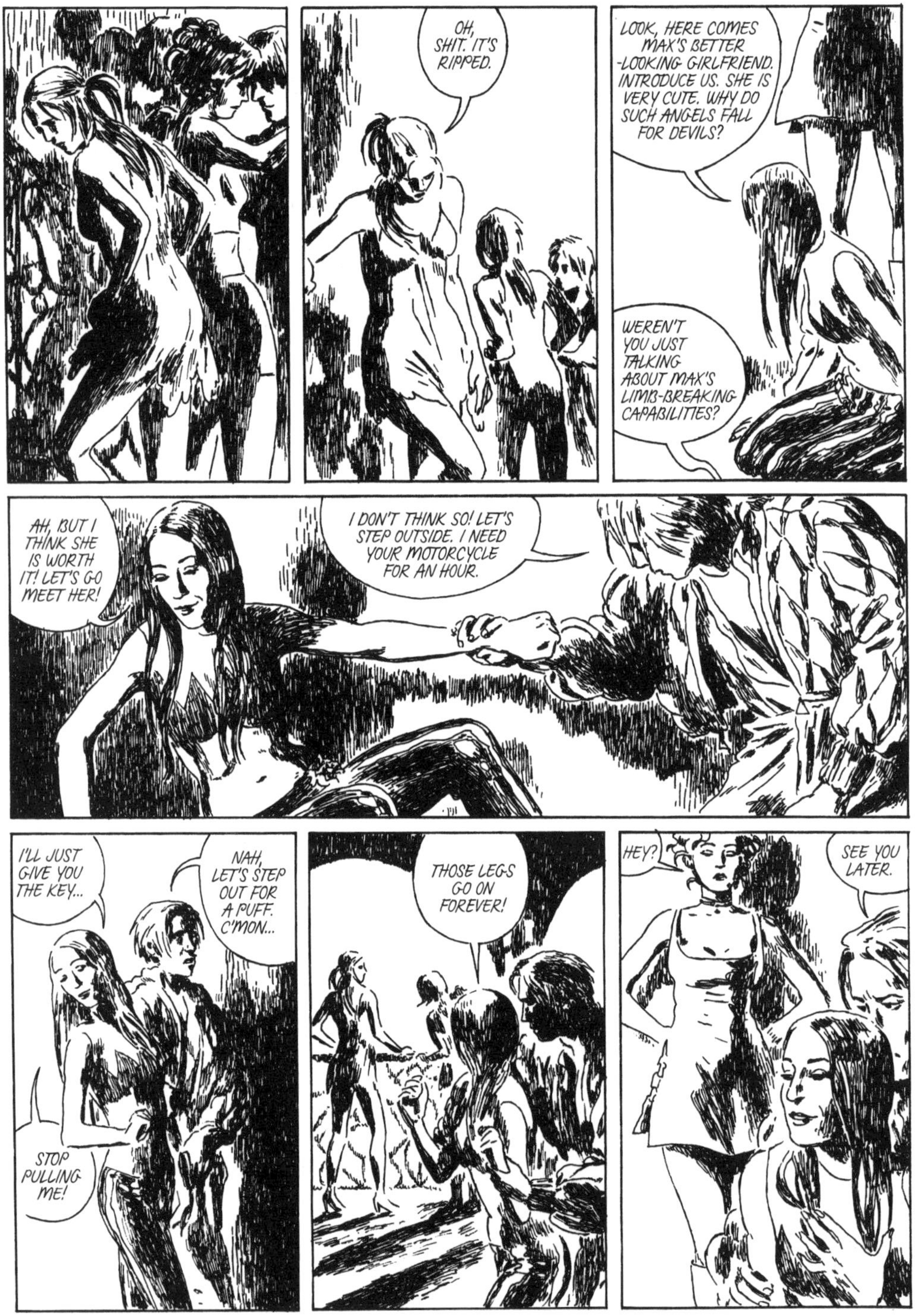
OH, SHIT. IT'S RIPPED.
LOOK, HERE COMES MAX'S BETTER -LOOKING GIRLFRIEND. INTRODUCE US. SHE IS VERY CUTE. WHY DO SUCH ANGELS FALL FOR DEVILS?
WEREN'T YOU JUST TALKING ABOUT MAX'S LIMB-BREAKING CAPABILITIES?
AH, BUT I THINK SHE IS WORTH IT! LET'S GO MEET HER!
I DON'T THINK SO! LET'S STEP OUTSIDE. I NEED YOUR MOTORCYCLE FOR AN HOUR.
I'LL JUST GIVE YOU THE KEY...
NAH, LET'S STEP OUT FOR A PUFF. C'MON...
STOP PULLING ME!
THOSE LEGS GO ON FOREVER!
HEY?
SEE YOU LATER.

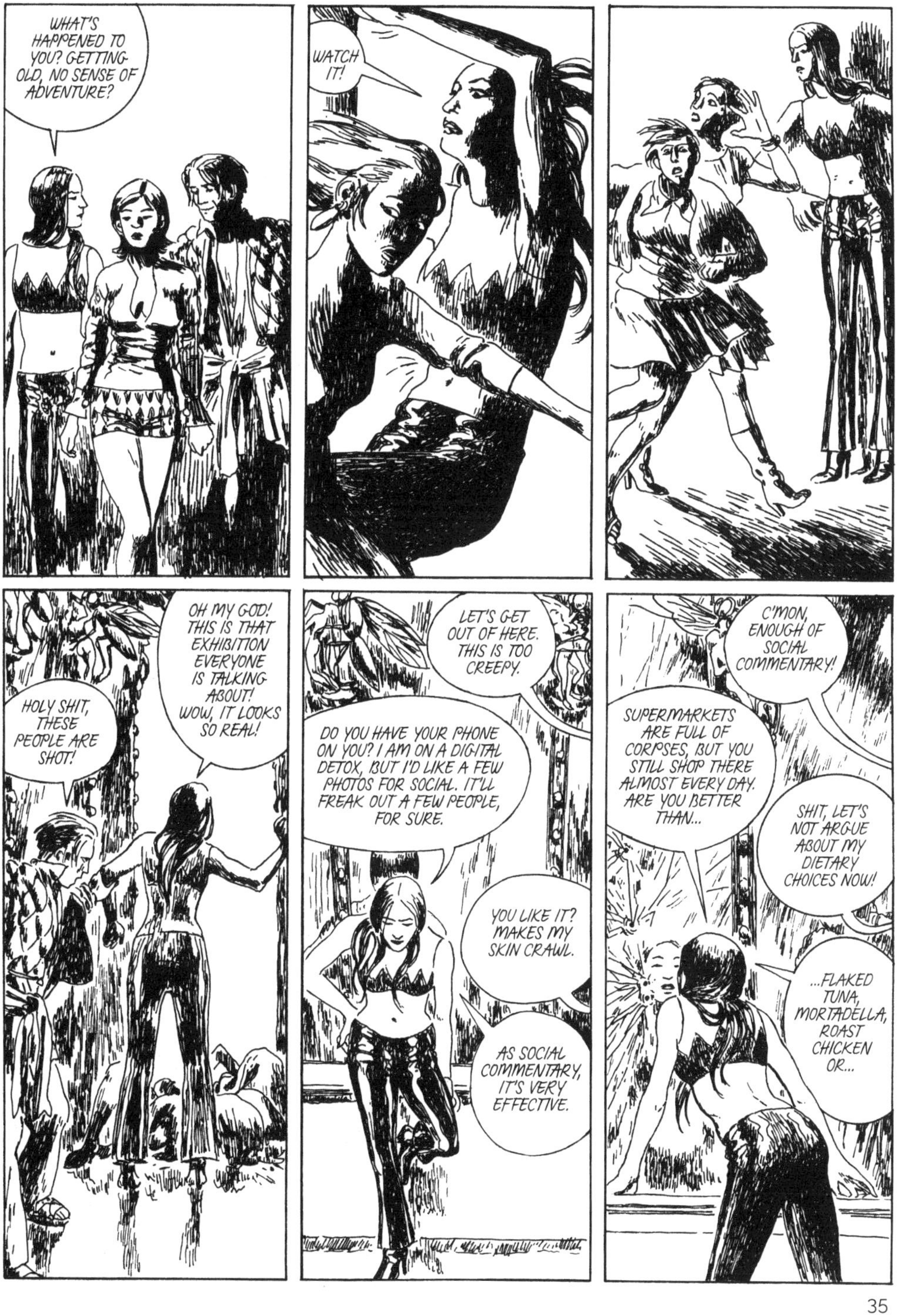
WHAT'S HAPPENED TO YOU? GETTING OLD, NO SENSE OF ADVENTURE?
WATCH IT!
OH MY GOD! THIS IS THAT EXHIBITION EVERYONE IS TALKING ABOUT! WOW, IT LOOKS SO REAL!
HOLY SHIT, THESE PEOPLE ARE SHOT!
LET'S GET OUT OF HERE. THIS IS TOO CREEPY.
DO YOU HAVE YOUR PHONE ON YOU? I AM ON A DIGITAL DETOX, BUT I'D LIKE A FEW PHOTOS FOR SOCIAL. IT'LL FREAK OUT A FEW PEOPLE, FOR SURE.
YOU LIKE IT? MAKES MY SKIN CRAWL.
AS SOCIAL COMMENTARY, IT'S VERY EFFECTIVE.
C'MON, ENOUGH OF SOCIAL COMMENTARY!
SUPERMARKETS ARE FULL OF CORPSES, BUT YOU STILL SHOP THERE ALMOST EVERY DAY. ARE YOU BETTER THAN...
SHIT, LET'S NOT ARGUE ABOUT MY DIETARY CHOICES NOW!
...FLAKED TUNA, MORTADELLA, ROAST CHICKEN OR...

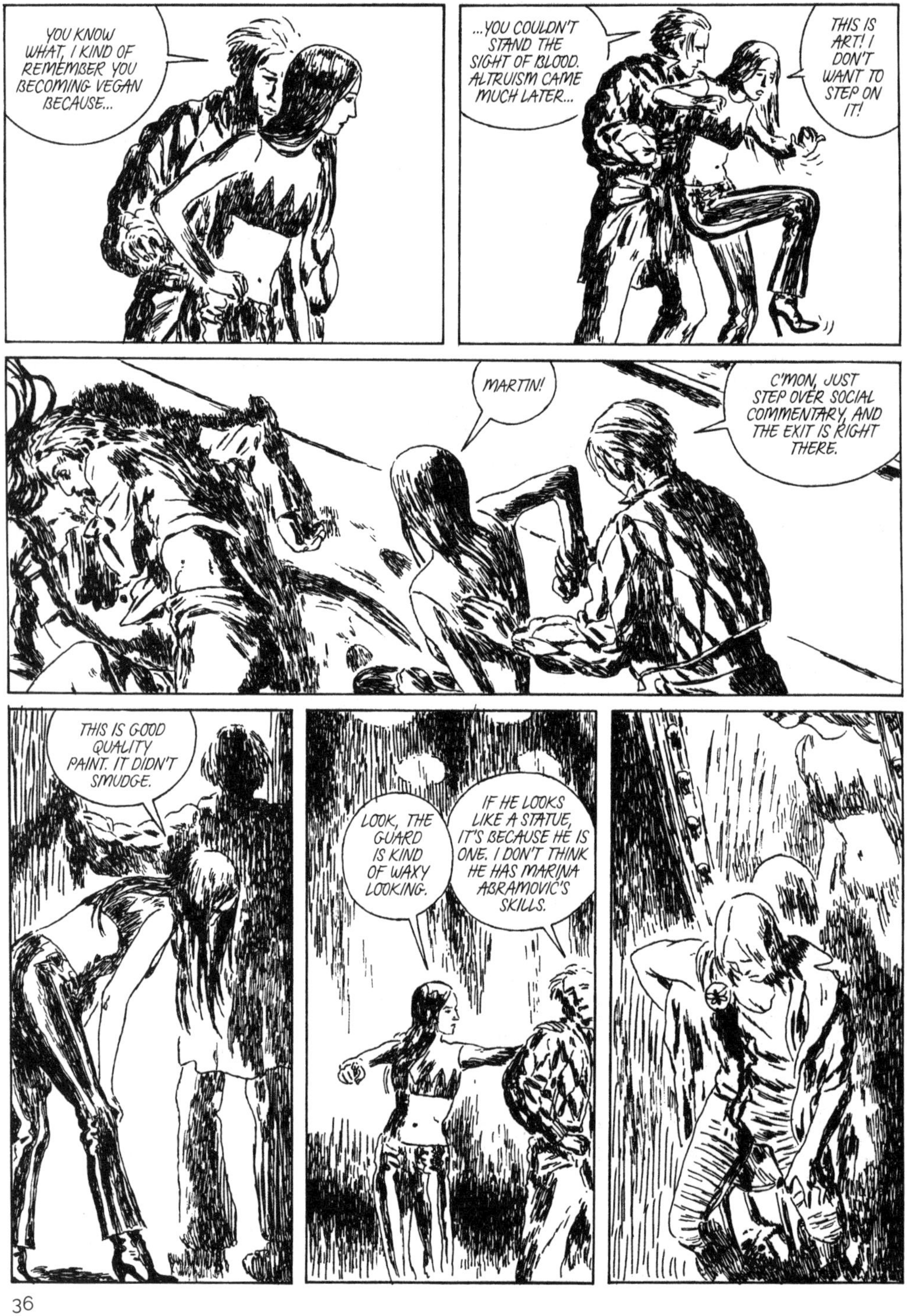
YOU KNOW WHAT, I KIND OF REMEMBER YOU BECOMING VEGAN BECAUSE...
...YOU COULDN'T STAND THE SIGHT OF BLOOD. ALTRUISM CAME MUCH LATER...
THIS IS ART! I DON'T WANT TO STEP ON IT!
MARTIN!
C'MON, JUST STEP OVER SOCIAL COMMENTARY, AND THE EXIT IS RIGHT THERE.
THIS IS GOOD QUALITY PAINT. IT DIDN'T SMUDGE.
LOOK, THE GUARD IS KIND OF WAXY LOOKING.
IF HE LOOKS LIKE A STATUE, IT'S BECAUSE HE IS ONE. I DON'T THINK HE HAS MARINA ABRAMOVIC'S SKILLS.

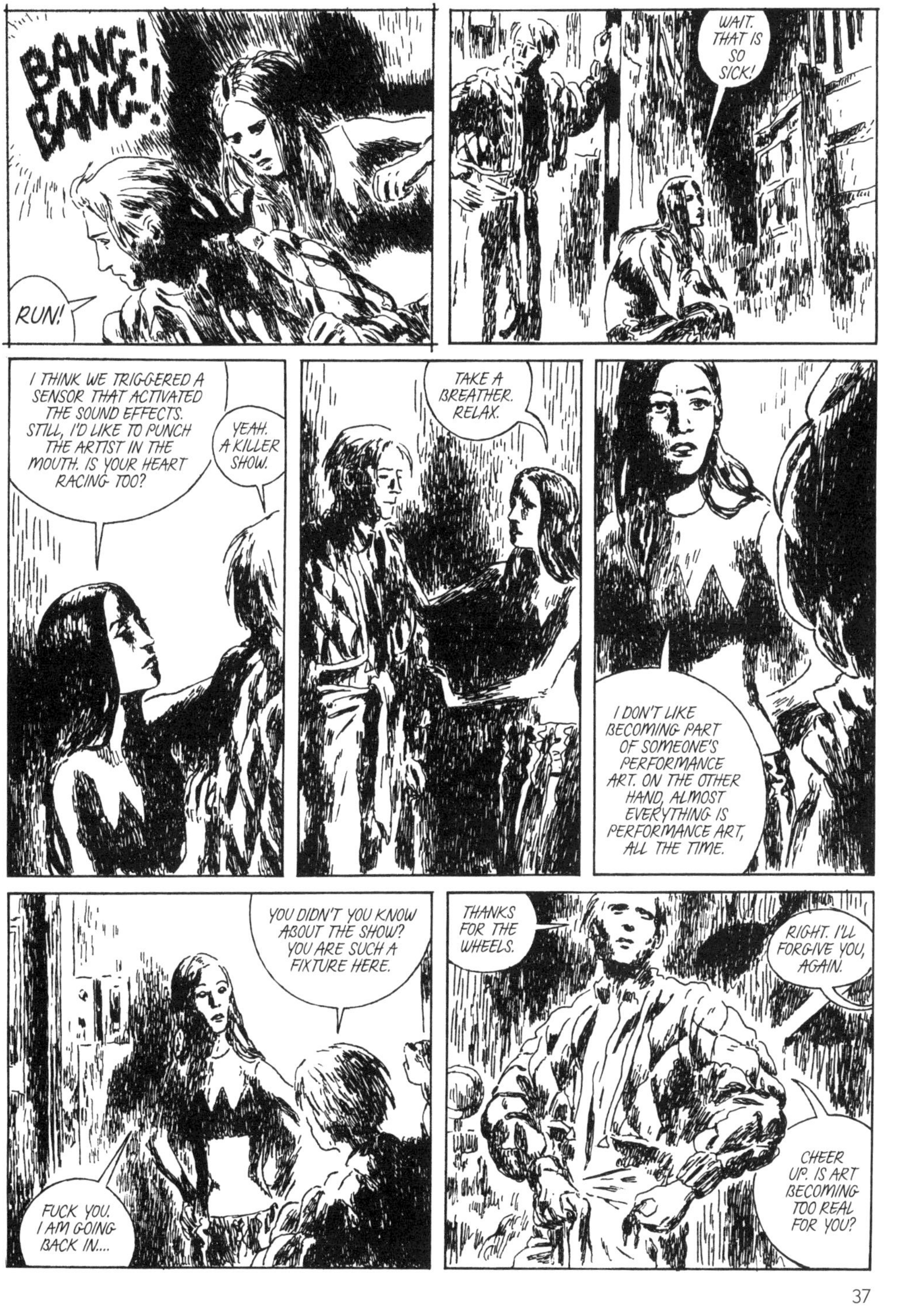
BANG! BANG!
RUN!
WAIT. THAT IS SO SICK!
I THINK WE TRIGGERED A SENSOR THAT ACTIVATED THE SOUND EFFECTS. STILL, I'D LIKE TO PUNCH THE ARTIST IN THE MOUTH. IS YOUR HEART RACING TOO?
YEAH. A KILLER SHOW.
TAKE A BREATHER. RELAX.
I DON'T LIKE BECOMING PART OF SOMEONE'S PERFORMANCE ART. ON THE OTHER HAND, ALMOST EVERYTHING IS PERFORMANCE ART, ALL THE TIME.
YOU DIDN'T YOU KNOW ABOUT THE SHOW? YOU ARE SUCH A FIXTURE HERE.
FUCK YOU. I AM GOING BACK IN....
THANKS FOR THE WHEELS.
RIGHT. I'LL FORGIVE YOU, AGAIN.
CHEER UP. IS ART BECOMING TOO REAL FOR YOU?

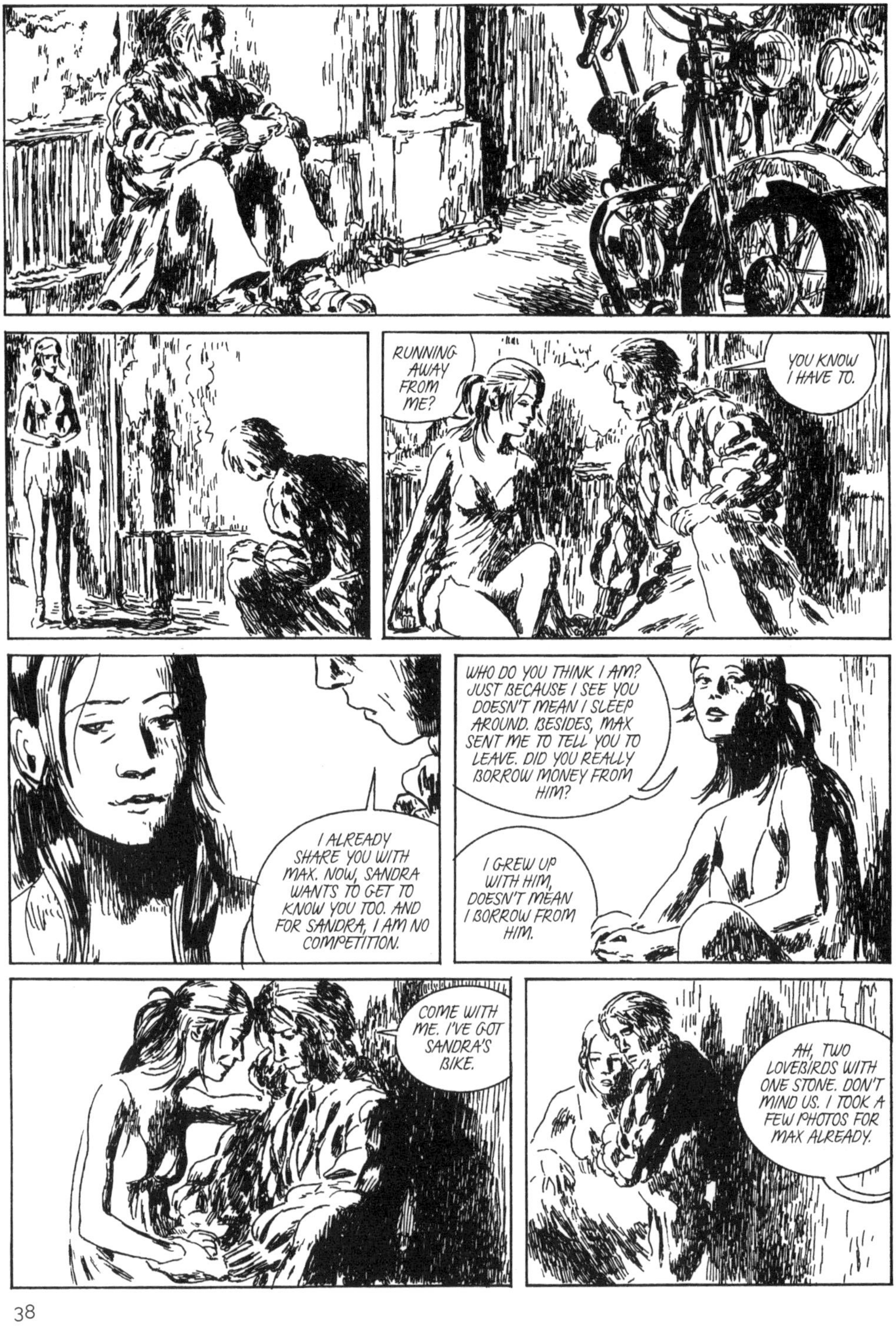
RUNNING AWAY FROM ME?
YOU KNOW I HAVE TO.
I ALREADY SHARE YOU WITH MAX. NOW, SANDRA WANTS TO GET TO KNOW YOU TOO. AND FOR SANDRA, I AM NO COMPETITION.
WHO DO YOU THINK I AM? JUST BECAUSE I SEE YOU DOESN'T MEAN I SLEEP AROUND. BESIDES, MAX SENT ME TO TELL YOU TO LEAVE. DID YOU REALLY BORROW MONEY FROM HIM?
I GREW UP WITH HIM, DOESN'T MEAN I BORROW FROM HIM.
COME WITH ME. I'VE GOT SANDRA'S BIKE.
AH, TWO LOVEBIRDS WITH ONE STONE. DON'T MIND US. I TOOK A FEW PHOTOS FOR MAX ALREADY.

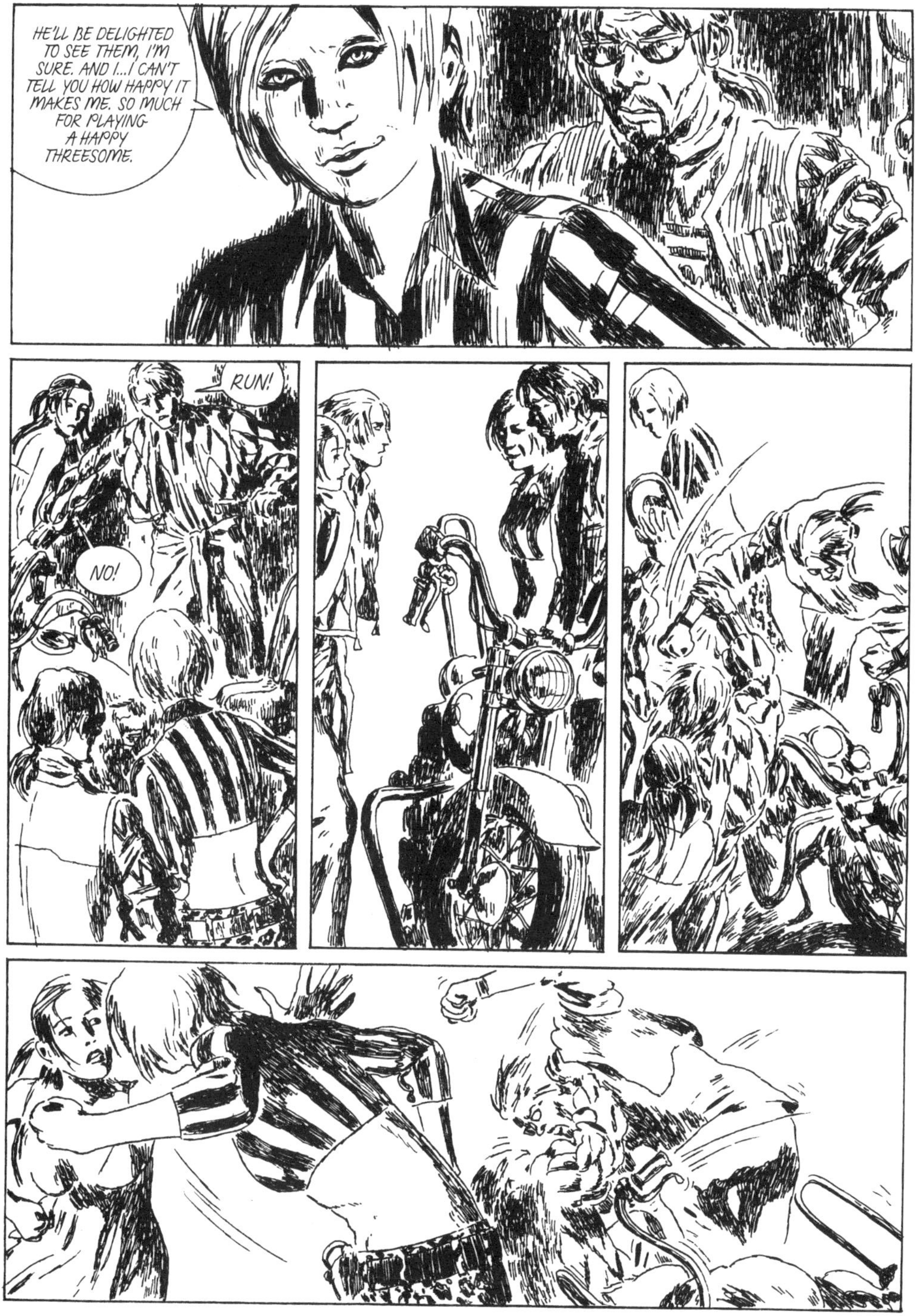
HE'LL BE DELIGHTED TO SEE THEM, I'M SURE. AND I...I CAN'T TELL YOU HOW HAPPY IT MAKES ME. SO MUCH FOR PLAYING A HAPPY THREESOME.
RUN!
NO!

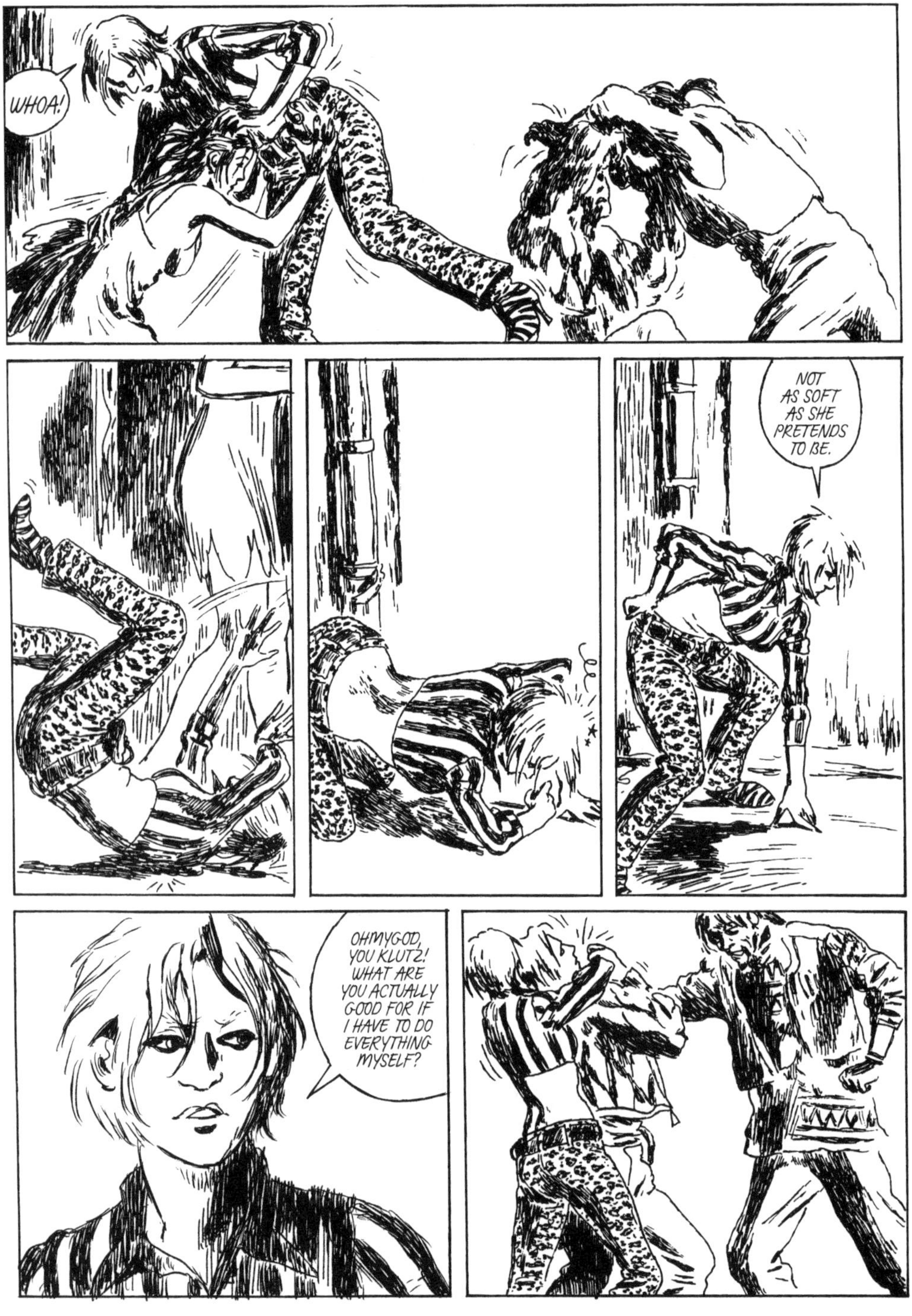
WHOA!
NOT AS SOFT AS SHE PRETENDS TO BE.
OHMYGOD, YOU KLUTZ! WHAT ARE YOU ACTUALLY GOOD FOR IF I HAVE TO DO EVERYTHING MYSELF?

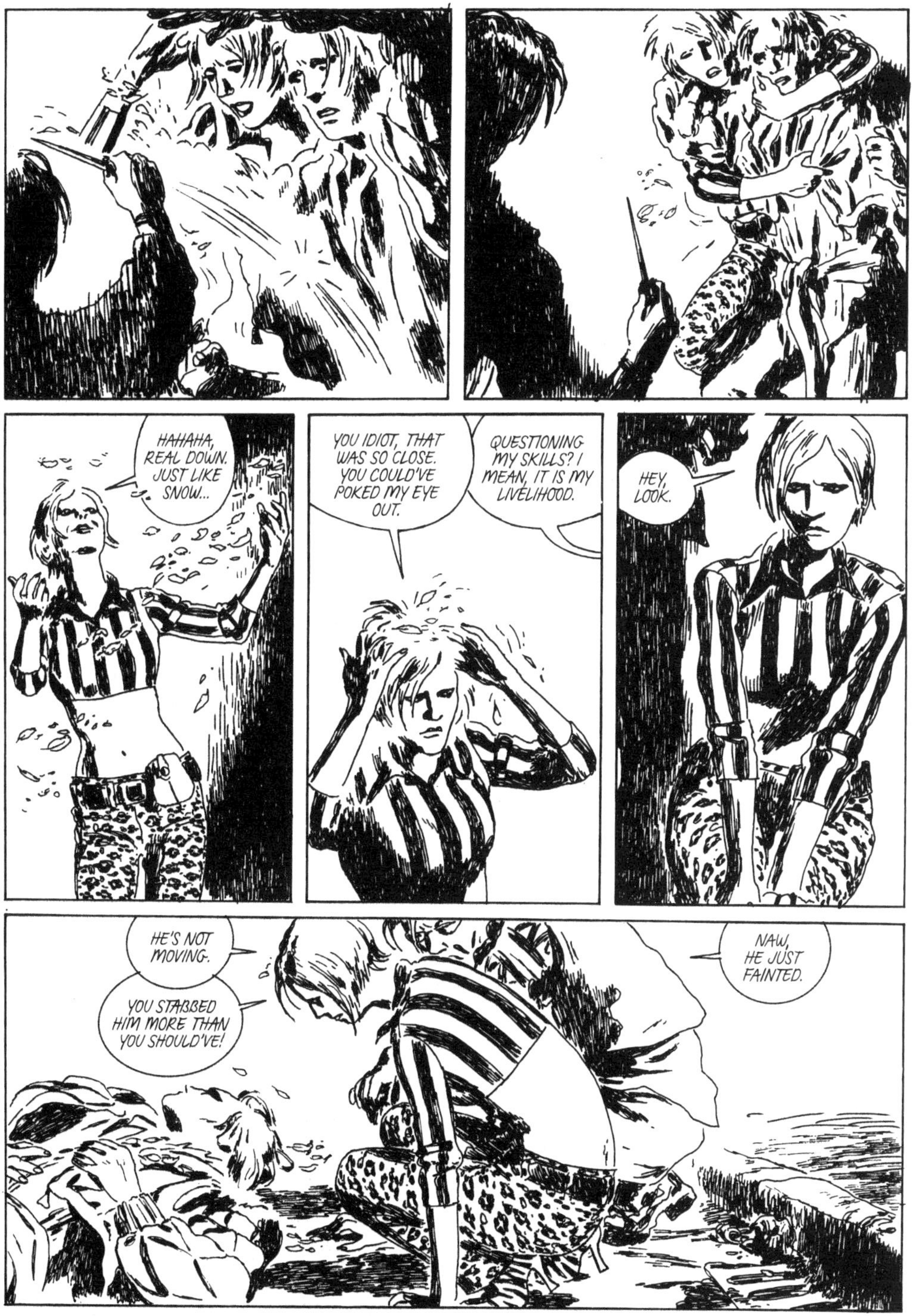
HAHAHA, REAL DOWN. JUST LIKE SNOW...
YOU IDIOT, THAT WAS SO CLOSE. YOU COULD'VE POKED MY EYE OUT.
QUESTIONING MY SKILLS? I MEAN, IT IS MY LIVELIHOOD.
HEY, LOOK.
HE'S NOT MOVING.
YOU STABBED HIM MORE THAN YOU SHOULD'VE!
NAW, HE JUST FAINTED.

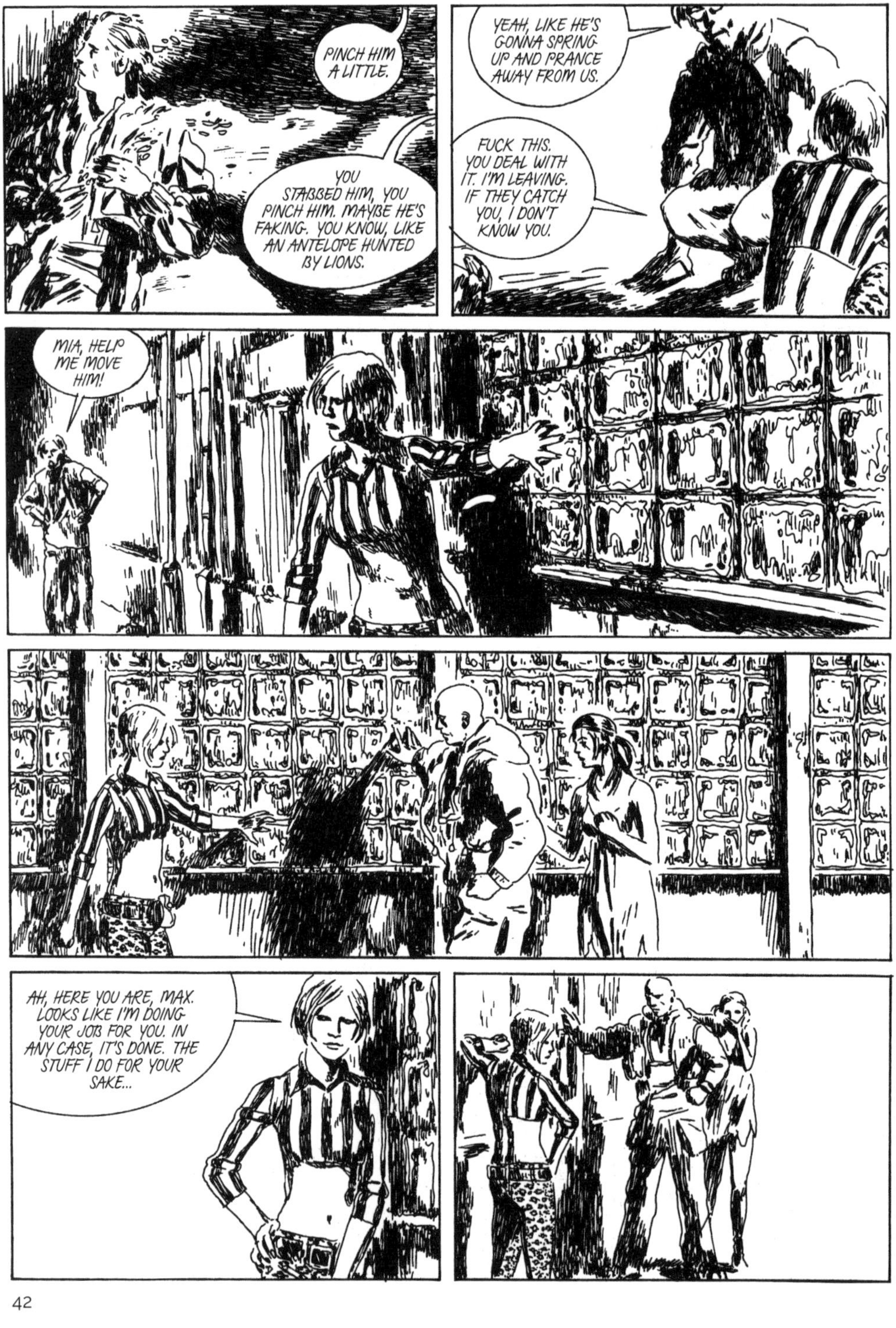
PINCH HIM A LITTLE.
YOU STABBED HIM, YOU PINCH HIM. MAYBE HE'S FAKING. YOU KNOW, LIKE AN ANTELOPE HUNTED BY LIONS.
YEAH, LIKE HE'S GONNA SPRING UP AND PRANCE AWAY FROM US.
FUCK THIS. YOU DEAL WITH IT. I'M LEAVING. IF THEY CATCH YOU, I DON'T KNOW YOU.
MIA, HELP ME MOVE HIM!
AH, HERE YOU ARE, MAX. LOOKS LIKE I'M DOING YOUR JOB FOR YOU. IN ANY CASE, IT'S DONE. THE STUFF I DO FOR YOUR SAKE...

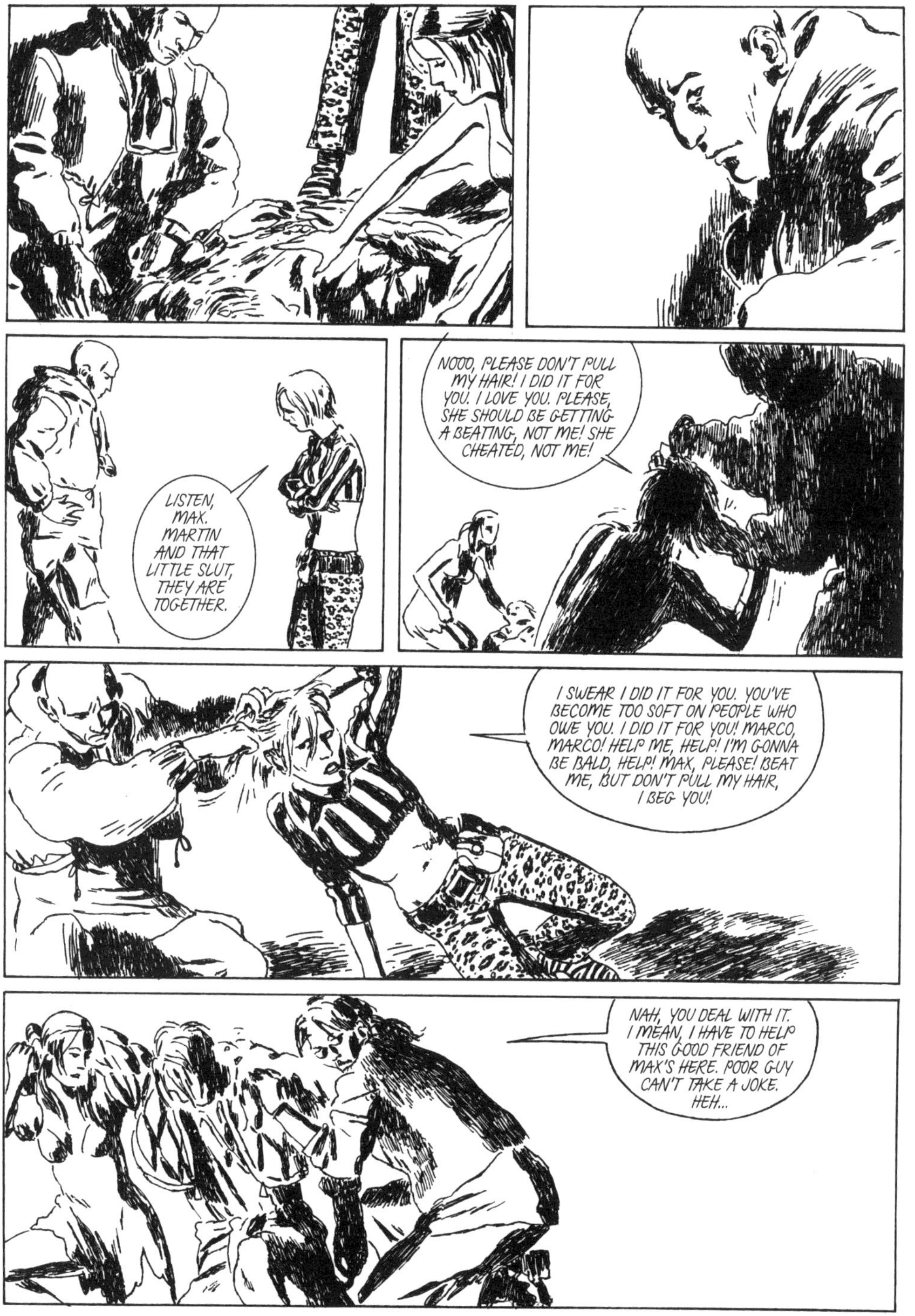
LISTEN, MAX. MARTIN AND THAT LITTLE SLUT, THEY ARE TOGETHER.
NOOO, PLEASE DON'T PULL MY HAIR! I DID IT FOR YOU. I LOVE YOU. PLEASE, SHE SHOULD BE GETTING A BEATING, NOT ME! SHE CHEATED, NOT ME!
I SWEAR I DID IT FOR YOU. YOU'VE BECOME TOO SOFT ON PEOPLE WHO OWE YOU. I DID IT FOR YOU! MARCO, MARCO! HELP ME, HELP! I'M GONNA BE BALD, HELP! MAX, PLEASE! BEAT ME, BUT DON'T PULL MY HAIR, I BEG YOU!
NAH, YOU DEAL WITH IT. I MEAN, I HAVE TO HELP THIS GOOD FRIEND OF MAX'S HERE. POOR GUY CAN'T TAKE A JOKE. HEH...

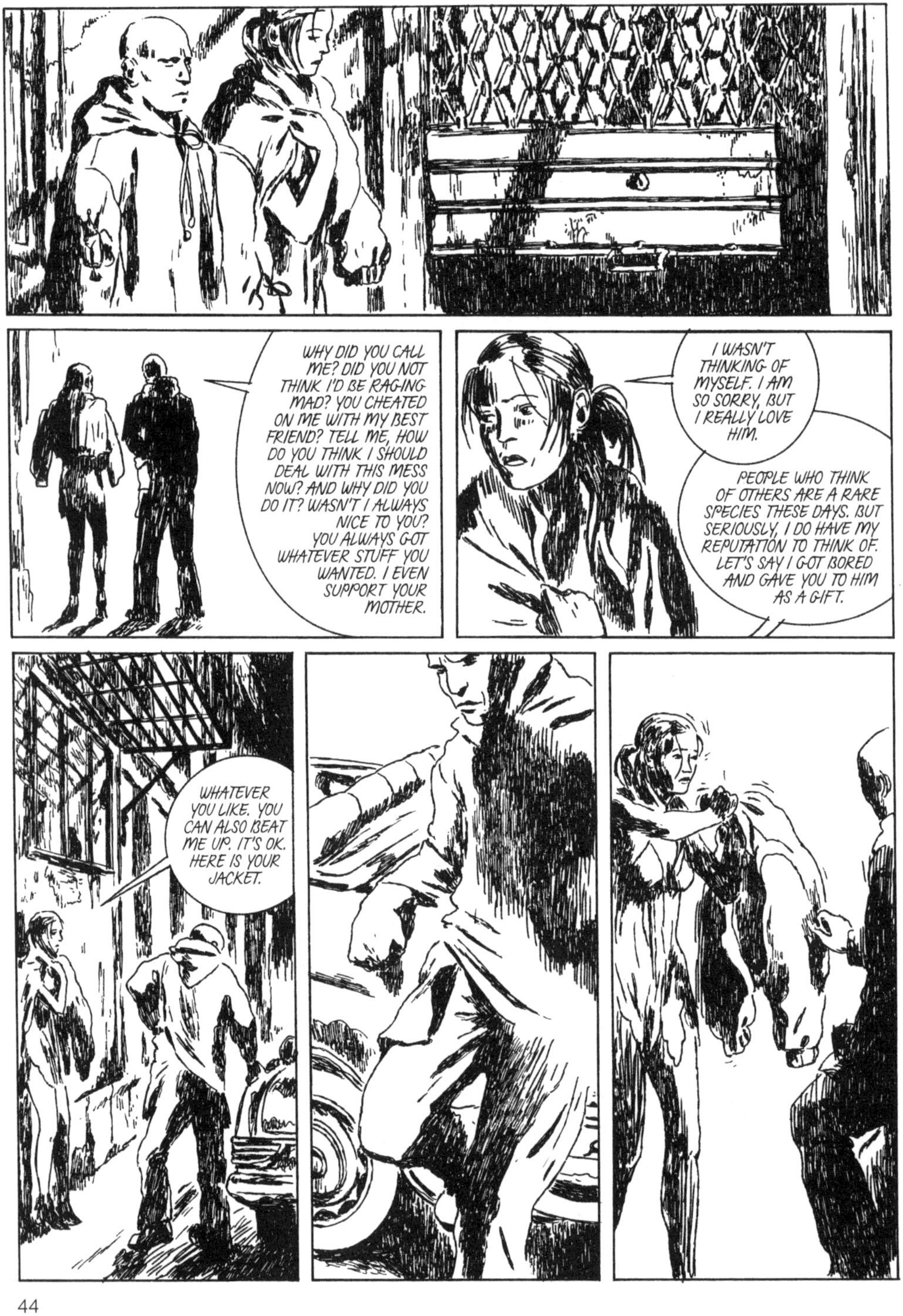
WHY DID YOU CALL ME? DID YOU NOT THINK I'D BE RAGING MAD? YOU CHEATED ON ME WITH MY BEST FRIEND? TELL ME, HOW DO YOU THINK I SHOULD DEAL WITH THIS MESS NOW? AND WHY DID YOU DO IT? WASN'T I ALWAYS NICE TO YOU? YOU ALWAYS GOT WHATEVER STUFF YOU WANTED. I EVEN SUPPORT YOUR MOTHER.
I WASN'T THINKING OF MYSELF. I AM SO SORRY, BUT I REALLY LOVE HIM.
PEOPLE WHO THINK OF OTHERS ARE A RARE SPECIES THESE DAYS. BUT SERIOUSLY, I DO HAVE MY REPUTATION TO THINK OF. LET'S SAY I GOT BORED AND GAVE YOU TO HIM AS A GIFT.
WHATEVER YOU LIKE. YOU CAN ALSO BEAT ME UP. IT'S OK. HERE IS YOUR JACKET.

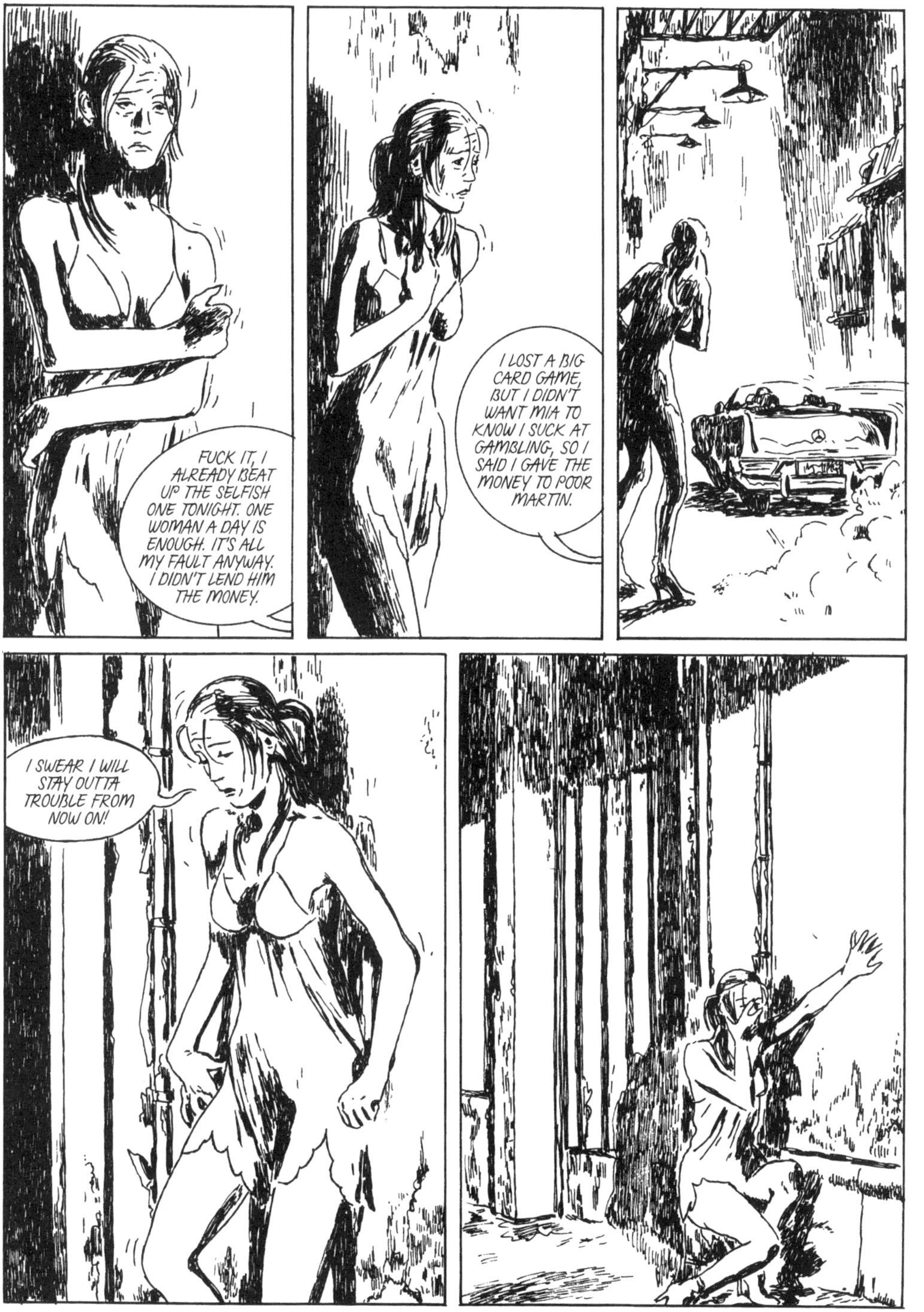
FUCK IT, I ALREADY BEAT UP THE SELFISH ONE TONIGHT. ONE WOMAN A DAY IS ENOUGH. IT'S ALL MY FAULT ANYWAY. I DIDN'T LEND HIM THE MONEY.
I LOST A BIG CARD GAME, BUT I DIDN'T WANT MIA TO KNOW I SUCK AT GAMBLING, SO I SAID I GAVE THE MONEY TO POOR MARTIN.
I SWEAR I WILL STAY OUTTA TROUBLE FROM NOW ON!

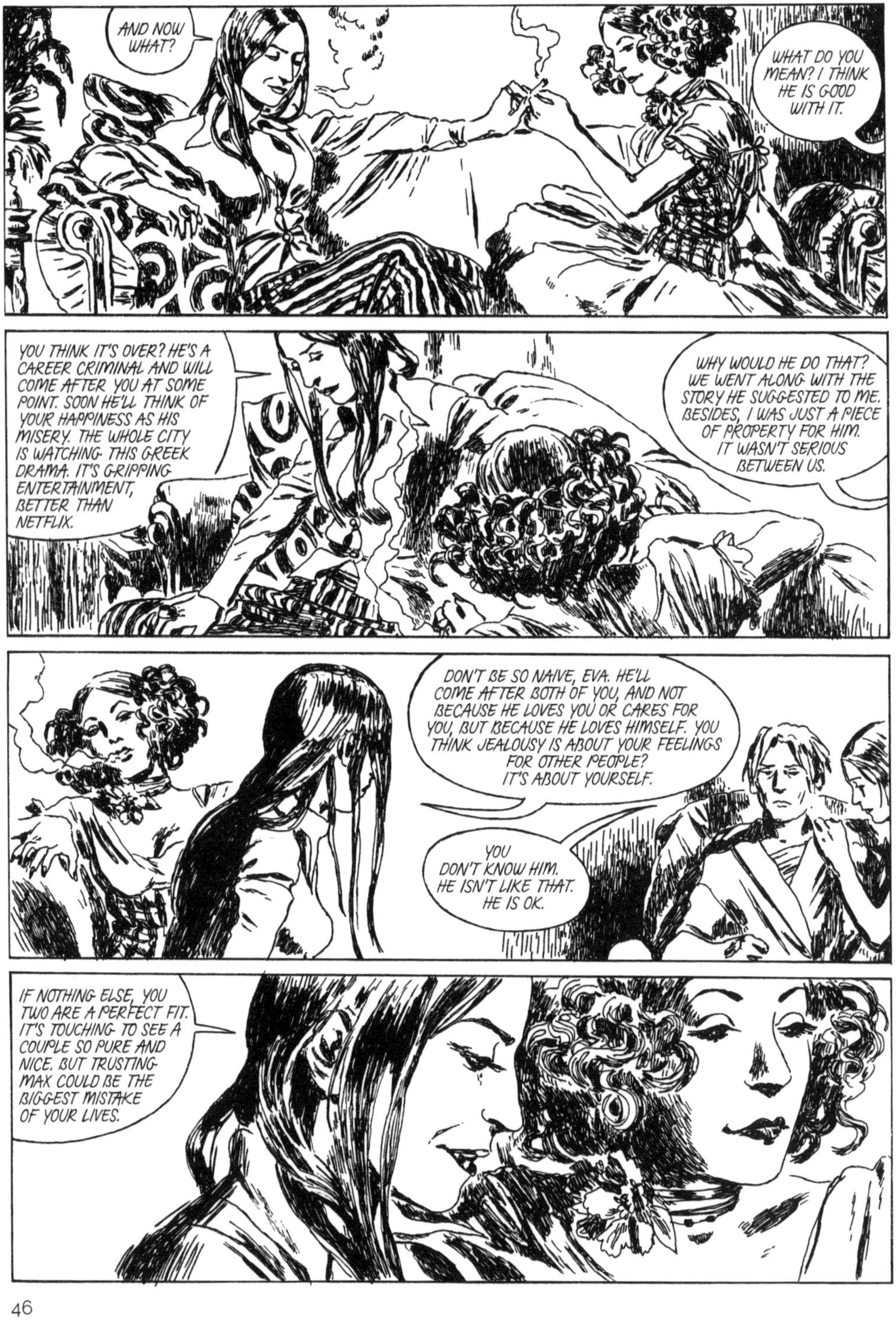
AND NOW WHAT?
WHAT DO YOU MEAN? I THINK HE IS GOOD WITH IT.
YOU THINK IT'S OVER? HE'S A CAREER CRIMINAL AND WILL COME AFTER YOU AT SOME POINT. SOON HE'LL THINK OF YOUR HAPPINESS AS HIS MISERY. THE WHOLE CITY IS WATCHING THIS GREEK DRAMA. IT'S GRIPPING ENTERTAINMENT, BETTER THAN NETFLIX.
WHY WOULD HE DO THAT? WE WENT ALONG WITH THE STORY HE SUGGESTED TO ME. BESIDES, I WAS JUST A PIECE OF PROPERTY FOR HIM. IT WASN'T SERIOUS BETWEEN US.
DON'T BE SO NAIVE, EVA. HE'LL COME AFTER BOTH OF YOU, AND NOT BECAUSE HE LOVES YOU OR CARES FOR YOU, BUT BECAUSE HE LOVES HIMSELF. YOU THINK JEALOUSY IS ABOUT YOUR FEELINGS FOR OTHER PEOPLE? IT'S ABOUT YOURSELF.
YOU DON'T KNOW HIM. HE ISN'T LIKE THAT. HE IS OK.
IF NOTHING ELSE, YOU TWO ARE A PERFECT FIT. IT'S TOUCHING TO SEE A COUPLE SO PURE AND NICE. BUT TRUSTING MAX COULD BE THE BIGGEST MISTAKE OF YOUR LIVES.

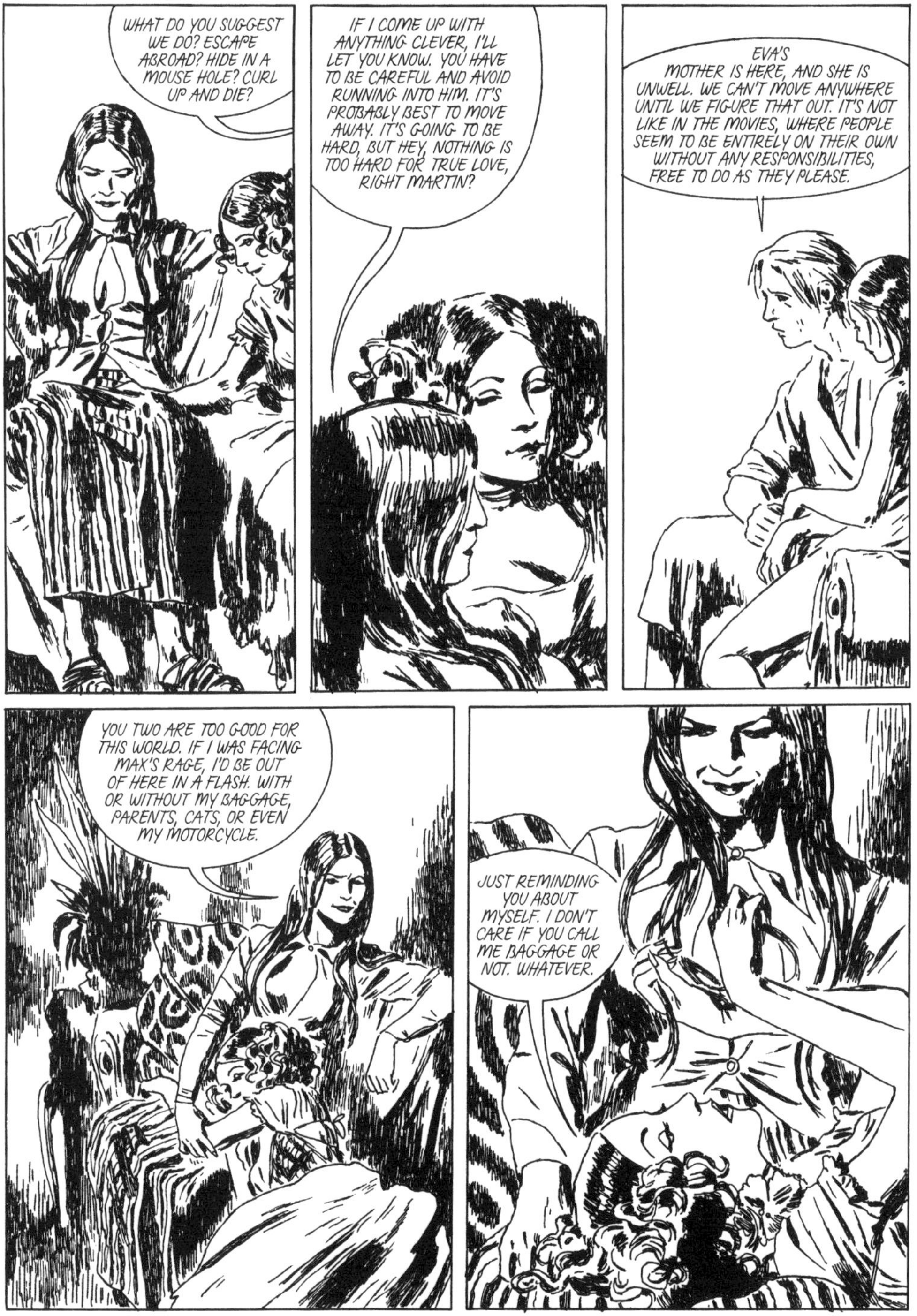
WHAT DO YOU SUGGEST WE DO? ESCAPE ABROAD? HIDE IN A MOUSE HOLE? CURL UP AND DIE?
IF I COME UP WITH ANYTHING CLEVER, I'LL LET YOU KNOW. YOU HAVE TO BE CAREFUL AND AVOID RUNNING INTO HIM. IT'S PROBABLY BEST TO MOVE AWAY. IT'S GOING TO BE HARD, BUT HEY, NOTHING IS TOO HARD FOR TRUE LOVE, RIGHT MARTIN?
EVA'S MOTHER IS HERE, AND SHE IS UNWELL. WE CAN'T MOVE ANYWHERE UNTIL WE FIGURE THAT OUT. IT'S NOT LIKE IN THE MOVIES, WHERE PEOPLE SEEM TO BE ENTIRELY ON THEIR OWN WITHOUT ANY RESPONSIBILITIES, FREE TO DO AS THEY PLEASE.
YOU TWO ARE TOO GOOD FOR THIS WORLD. IF I WAS FACING MAX'S RAGE, I'D BE OUT OF HERE IN A FLASH. WITH OR WITHOUT MY BAGGAGE, PARENTS, CATS, OR EVEN MY MOTORCYCLE.
JUST REMINDING YOU ABOUT MYSELF. I DON'T CARE IF YOU CALL ME BAGGAGE OR NOT. WHATEVER.

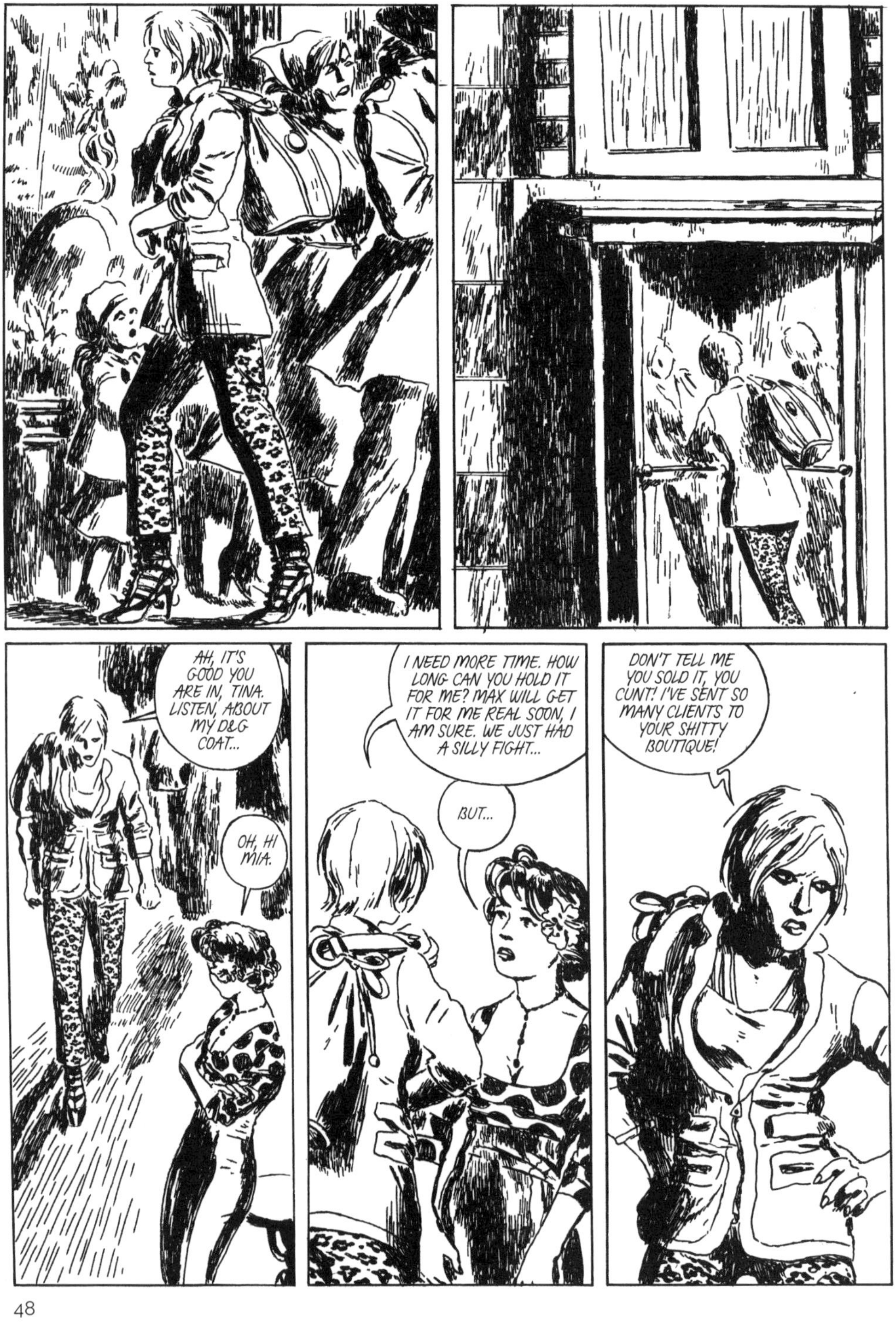
AH, IT'S GOOD YOU ARE IN, TINA. LISTEN, ABOUT MY D&G COAT...
OH, HI MIA.
I NEED MORE TIME. HOW LONG CAN YOU HOLD IT FOR ME? MAX WILL GET IT FOR ME REAL SOON, I AM SURE. WE JUST HAD A SILLY FIGHT...
BUT...
DON'T TELL ME YOU SOLD IT, YOU CUNT! I'VE SENT SO MANY CLIENTS TO YOUR SHITTY BOUTIQUE!

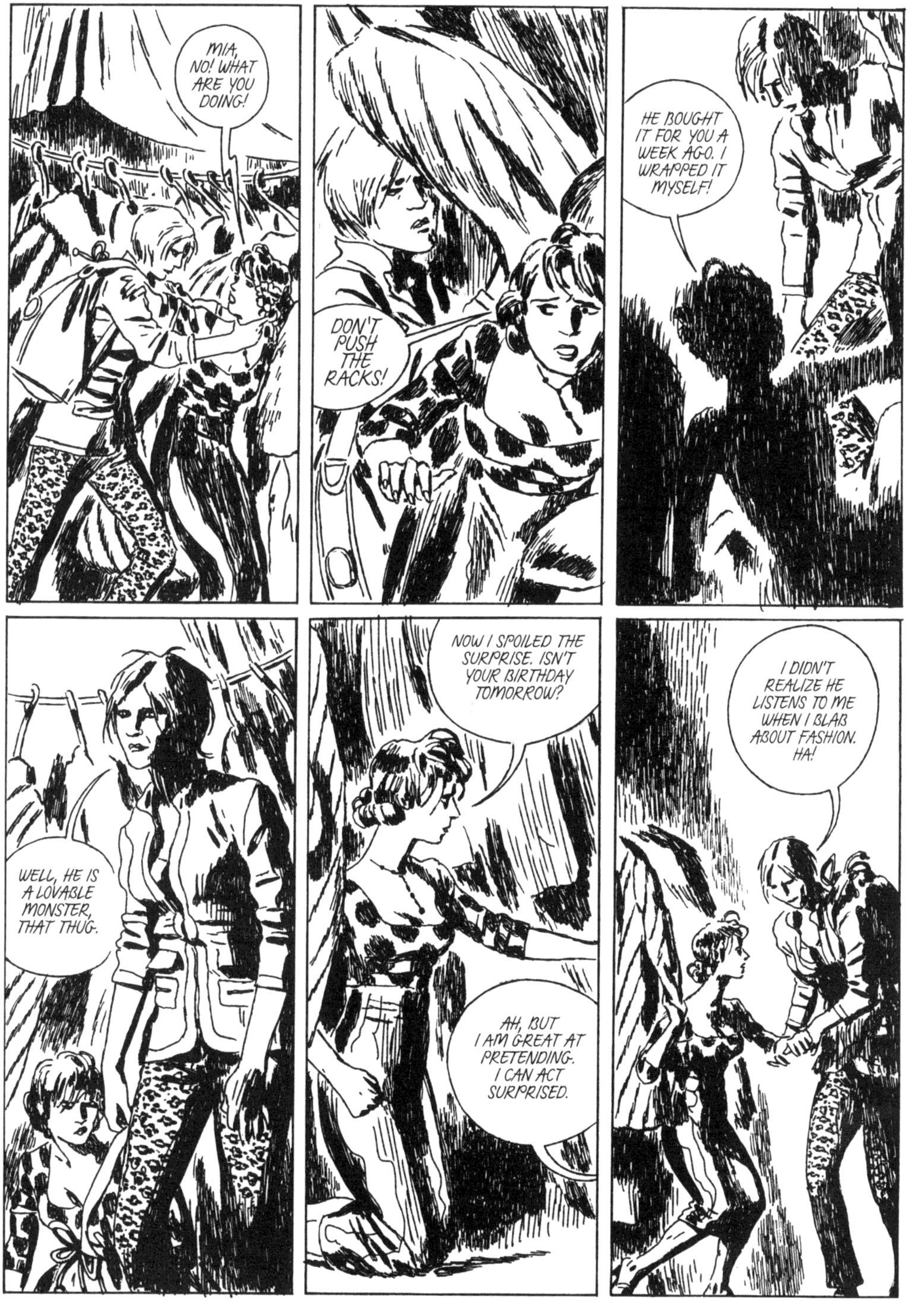
MIA, NO! WHAT ARE YOU DOING!
DON'T PUSH THE RACKS!
HE BOUGHT IT FOR YOU A WEEK AGO. I WRAPPED IT MYSELF!
WELL, HE IS A LOVABLE MONSTER, THAT THUG.
NOW I SPOILED THE SURPRISE. ISN'T YOUR BIRTHDAY TOMORROW?
AH, BUT I AM GREAT AT PRETENDING. I CAN ACT SURPRISED.
I DIDN'T REALIZE HE LISTENS TO ME WHEN I BLAB ABOUT FASHION. HA!

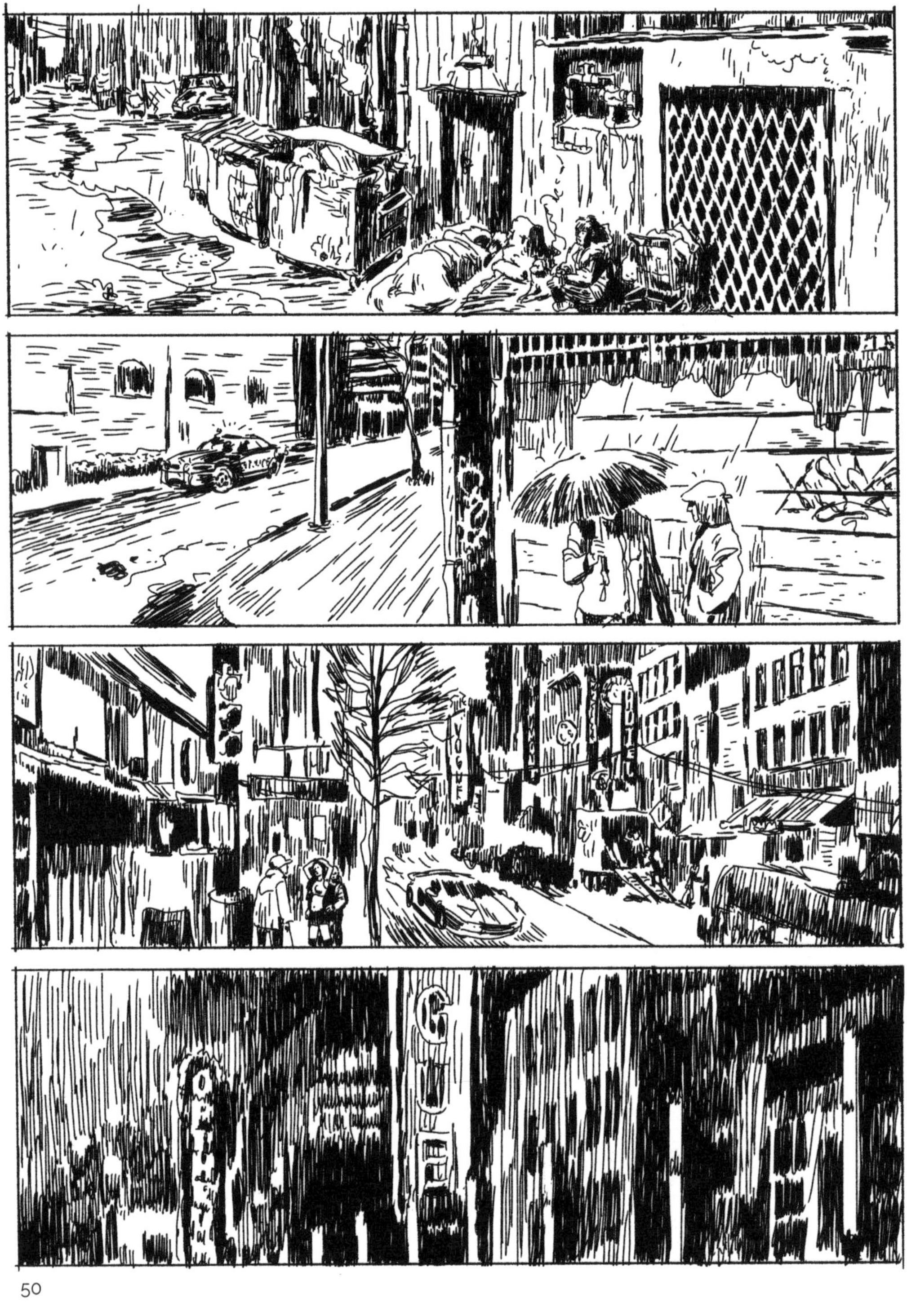
VOGUE
HOTEL

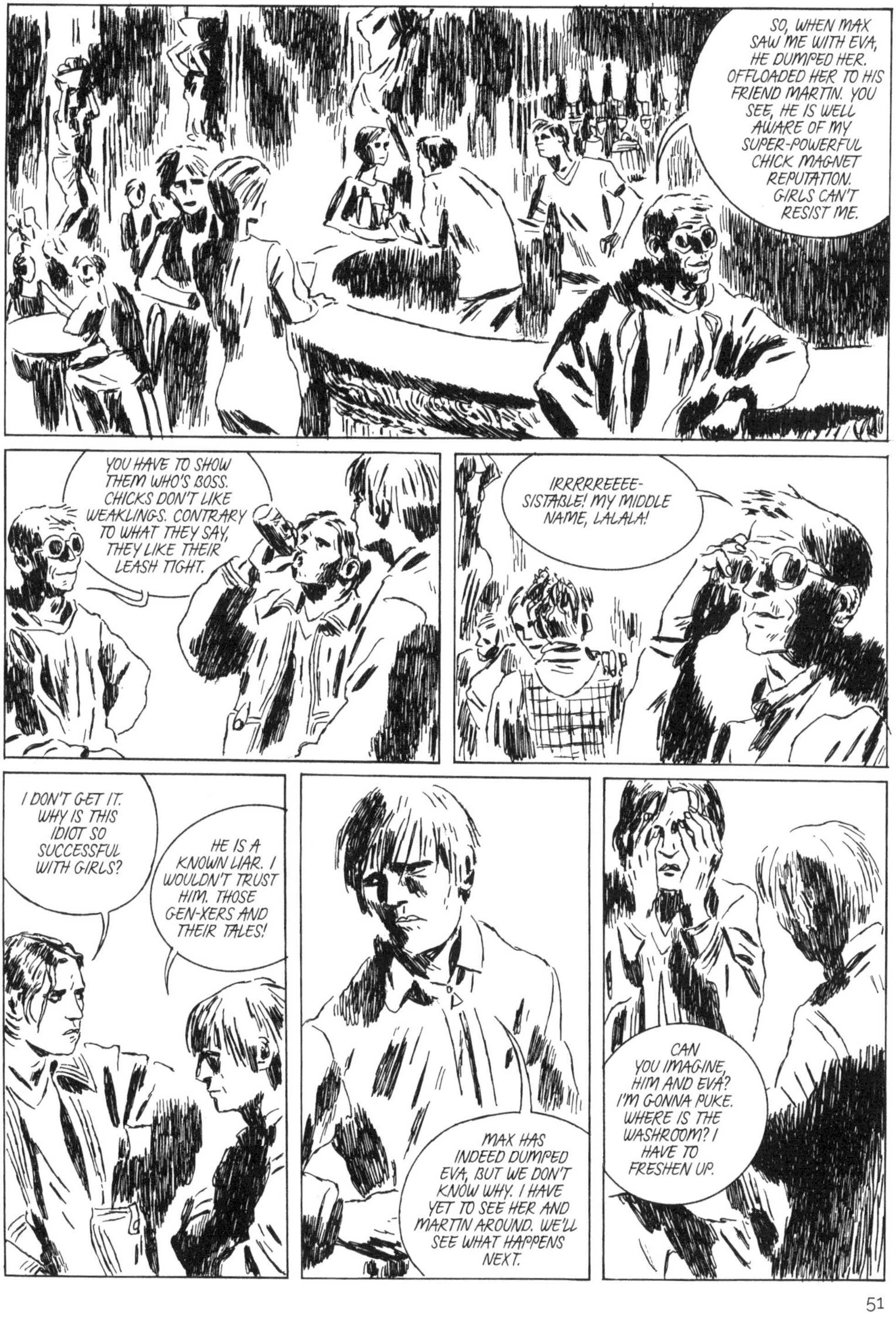
SO, WHEN MAX SAW ME WITH EVA, HE DUMPED HER. OFFLOADED HER TO HIS FRIEND MARTIN. YOU SEE, HE IS WELL AWARE OF MY SUPER-POWERFUL CHICK MAGNET REPUTATION. GIRLS CAN'T RESIST ME.
YOU HAVE TO SHOW THEM WHO'S BOSS. CHICKS DON'T LIKE WEAKLINGS. CONTRARY TO WHAT THEY SAY, THEY LIKE THEIR LEASH TIGHT.
IRRRRREEEE-SISTABLE! MY MIDDLE NAME, LALALA!
I DON'T GET IT. WHY IS THIS IDIOT SO SUCCESSFUL WITH GIRLS?
HE IS A KNOWN LIAR. I WOULDN'T TRUST HIM. THOSE GEN-XERS AND THEIR TALES!
MAX HAS INDEED DUMPED EVA, BUT WE DON'T KNOW WHY. I HAVE YET TO SEE HER AND MARTIN AROUND. WE'LL SEE WHAT HAPPENS NEXT.
CAN YOU IMAGINE, HIM AND EVA? I'M GONNA PUKE. WHERE IS THE WASHROOM? I HAVE TO FRESHEN UP.

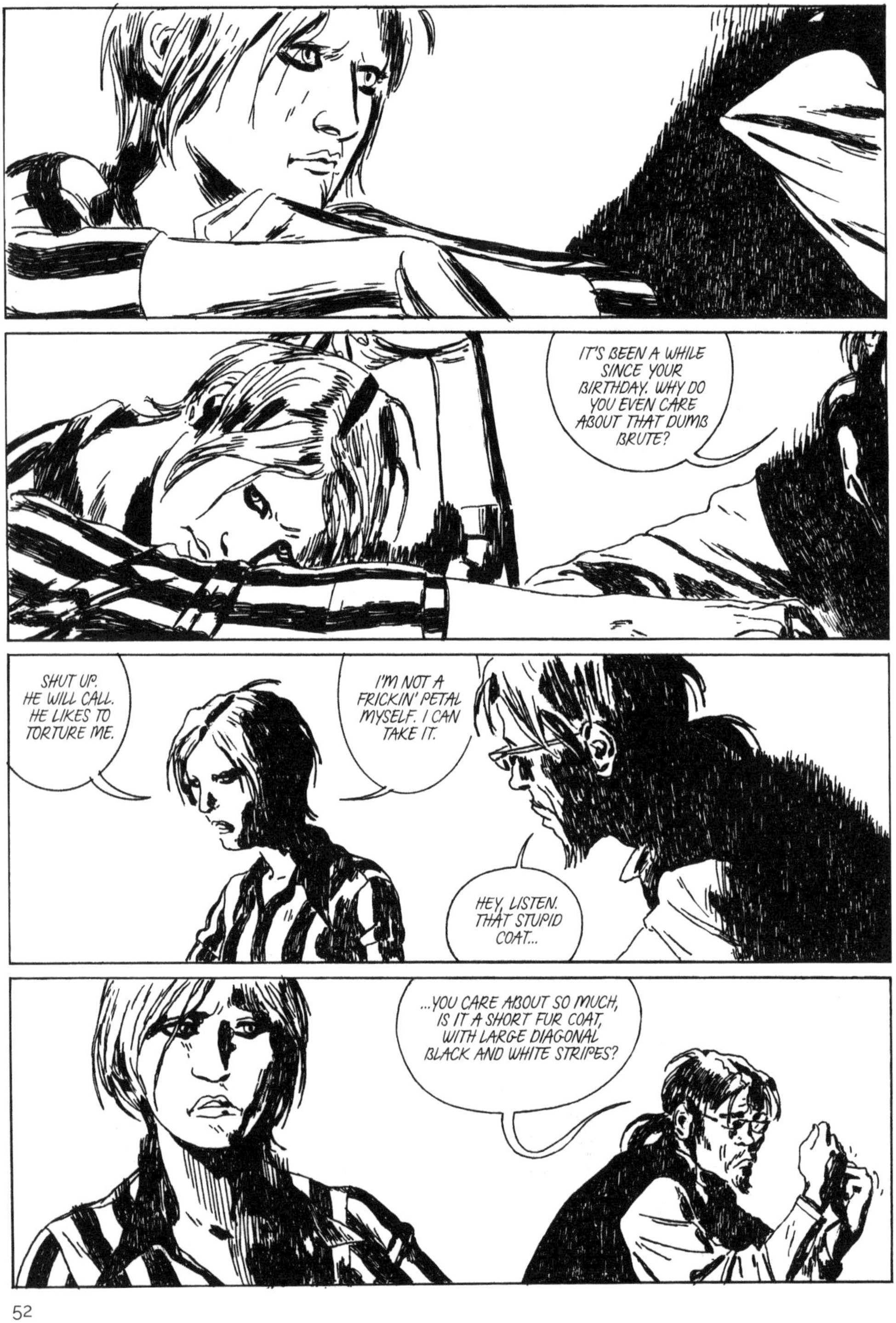
IT'S BEEN A WHILE SINCE YOUR BIRTHDAY. WHY DO YOU EVEN CARE ABOUT THAT DUMB BRUTE?
SHUT UP. HE WILL CALL. HE LIKES TO TORTURE ME.
I'M NOT A FRICKIN' PETAL MYSELF. I CAN TAKE IT.
HEY, LISTEN. THAT STUPID COAT...
...YOU CARE ABOUT SO MUCH, IS IT A SHORT FUR COAT, WITH LARGE DIAGONAL BLACK AND WHITE STRIPES?

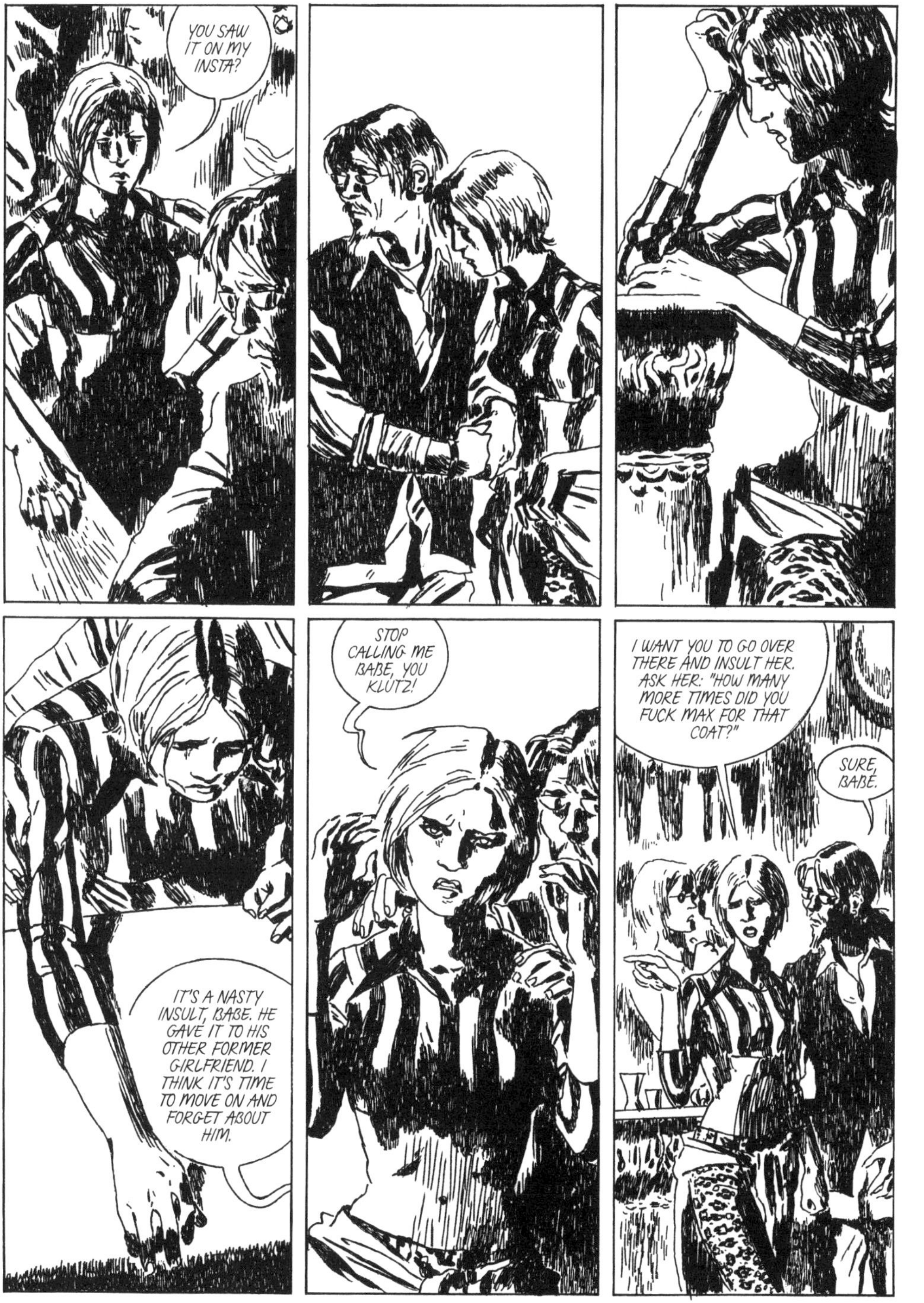
YOU SAW IT ON MY INSTA?
IT'S A NASTY INSULT, BABE. HE GAVE IT TO HIS OTHER FORMER GIRLFRIEND. I THINK IT'S TIME TO MOVE ON AND FORGET ABOUT HIM.
STOP CALLING ME BABE, YOU KLUTZ!
I WANT YOU TO GO OVER THERE AND INSULT HER. ASK HER: "HOW MANY MORE TIMES DID YOU FUCK MAX FOR THAT COAT?"
SURE, BABE.

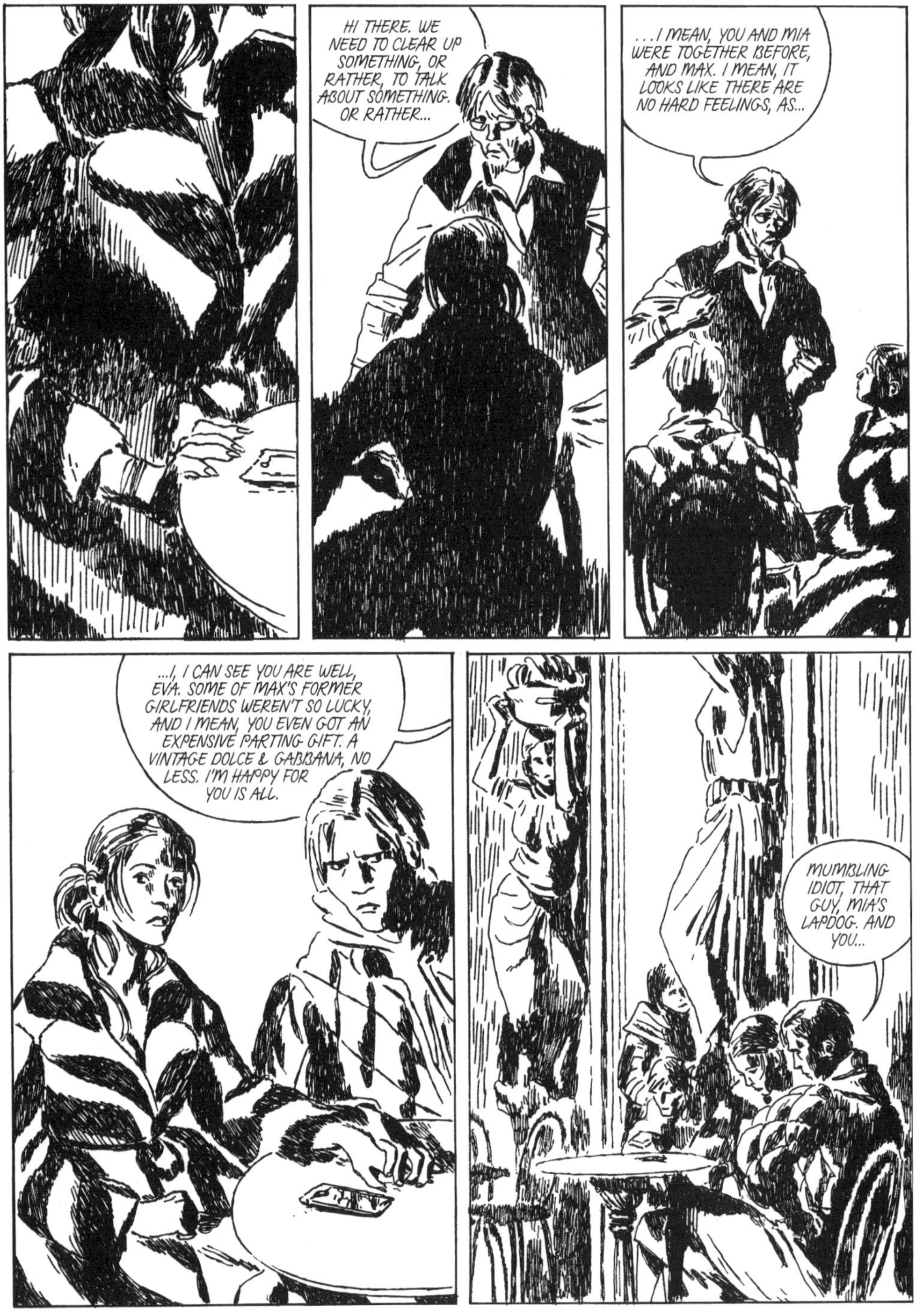
HI THERE. WE NEED TO CLEAR UP SOMETHING, OR RATHER, TO TALK ABOUT SOMETHING. OR RATHER...
. . . I MEAN, YOU AND MIA WERE TOGETHER BEFORE, AND MAX. I MEAN, IT LOOKS LIKE THERE ARE NO HARD FEELINGS, AS...
...I, I CAN SEE YOU ARE WELL, EVA. SOME OF MAX'S FORMER GIRLFRIENDS WEREN'T SO LUCKY, AND I MEAN, YOU EVEN GOT AN EXPENSIVE PARTING GIFT. A VINTAGE DOLCE & GABBANA, NO LESS. I'M HAPPY FOR YOU IS ALL.
MUMBLING IDIOT, THAT GUY, MIA'S LAPDOG. AND YOU...

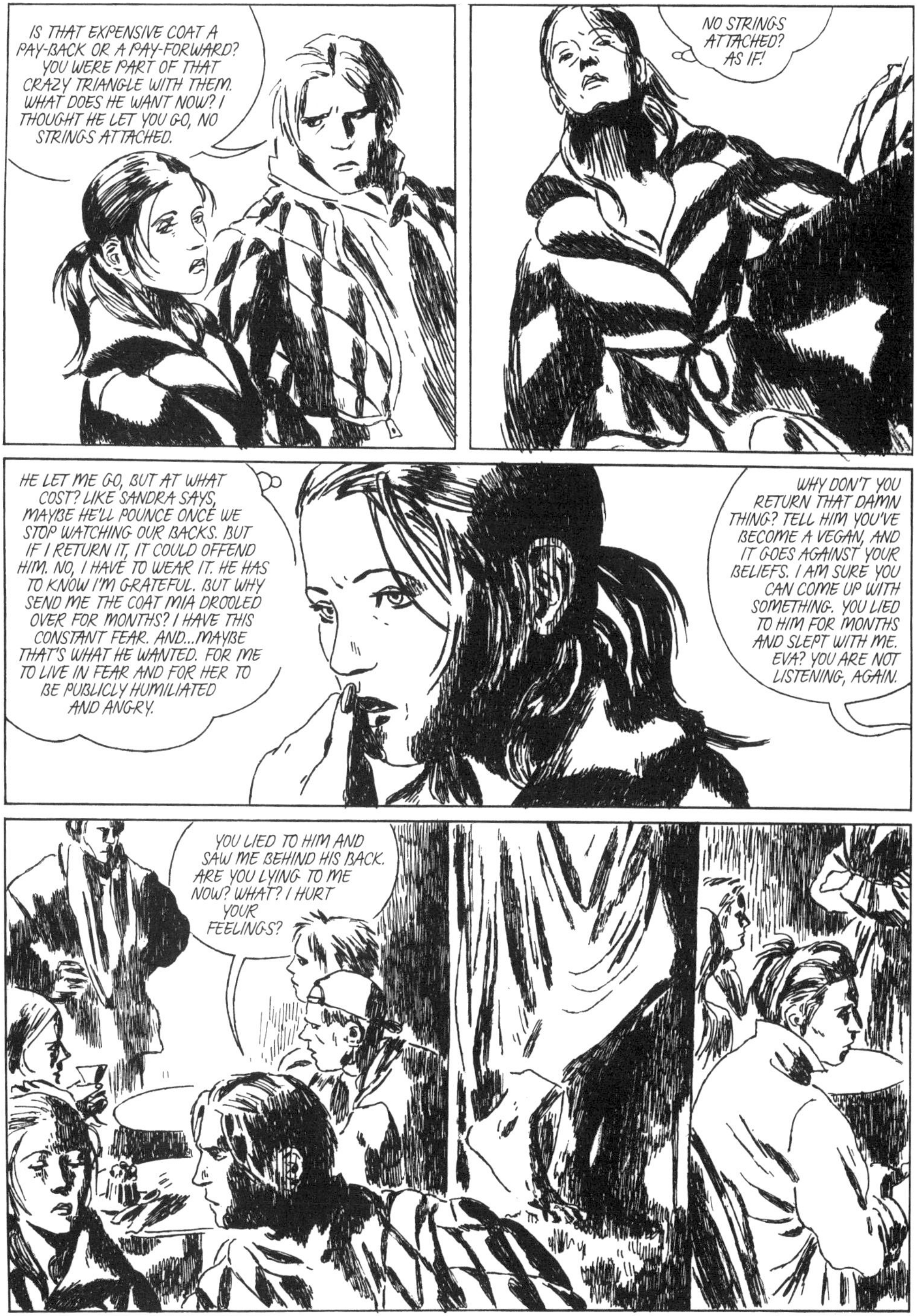
IS THAT EXPENSIVE COAT A PAY-BACK OR A PAY-FORWARD? YOU WERE PART OF THAT CRAZY TRIANGLE WITH THEM. WHAT DOES HE WANT NOW? I THOUGHT HE LET YOU GO, NO STRINGS ATTACHED.
NO STRINGS ATTACHED? AS IF!
HE LET ME GO, BUT AT WHAT COST? LIKE SANDRA SAYS, MAYBE HE'LL POUNCE ONCE WE STOP WATCHING OUR BACKS. BUT IF I RETURN IT, IT COULD OFFEND HIM. NO, I HAVE TO WEAR IT. HE HAS TO KNOW I'M GRATEFUL. BUT WHY SEND ME THE COAT MIA DROOLED OVER FOR MONTHS? I HAVE THIS CONSTANT FEAR. AND...MAYBE THAT'S WHAT HE WANTED. FOR ME TO LIVE IN FEAR AND FOR HER TO BE PUBLICLY HUMILIATED AND ANGRY.
WHY DON'T YOU RETURN THAT DAMN THING? TELL HIM YOU'VE BECOME A VEGAN, AND IT GOES AGAINST YOUR BELIEFS. I AM SURE YOU CAN COME UP WITH SOMETHING. YOU LIED TO HIM FOR MONTHS AND SLEPT WITH ME. EVA? YOU ARE NOT LISTENING, AGAIN.
YOU LIED TO HIM AND SAW ME BEHIND HIS BACK. ARE YOU LYING TO ME NOW? WHAT? I HURT YOUR FEELINGS?

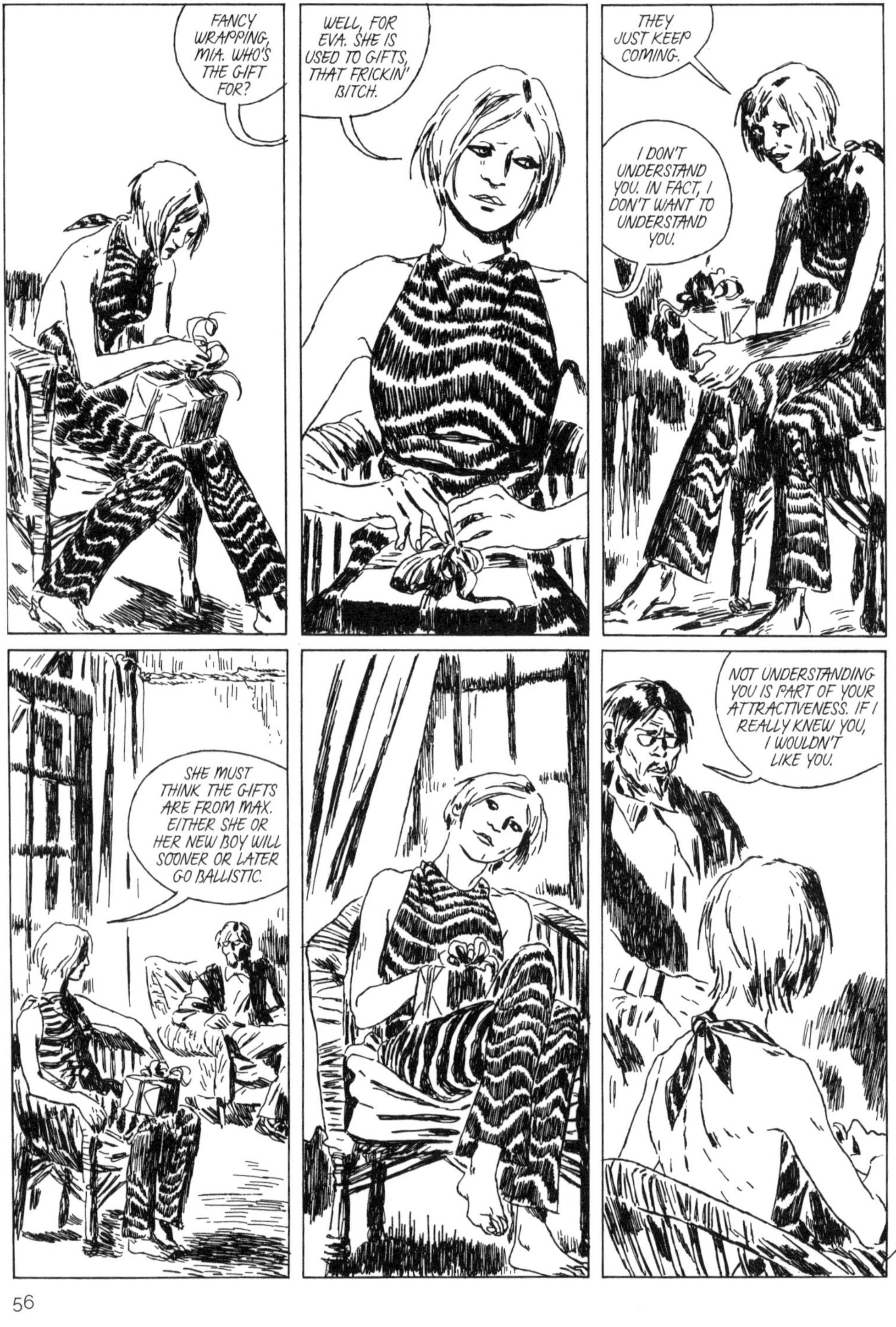
FANCY WRAPPING, MIA. WHO'S THE GIFT FOR?
WELL, FOR EVA. SHE IS USED TO GIFTS, THAT FRICKIN' BITCH.
THEY JUST KEEP COMING.
I DON'T UNDERSTAND YOU. IN FACT, I DON'T WANT TO UNDERSTAND YOU.
SHE MUST THINK THE GIFTS ARE FROM MAX. EITHER SHE OR HER NEW BOY WILL SOONER OR LATER GO BALLISTIC.
NOT UNDERSTANDING YOU IS PART OF YOUR ATTRACTIVENESS. IF I REALLY KNEW YOU, I WOULDN'T LIKE YOU.

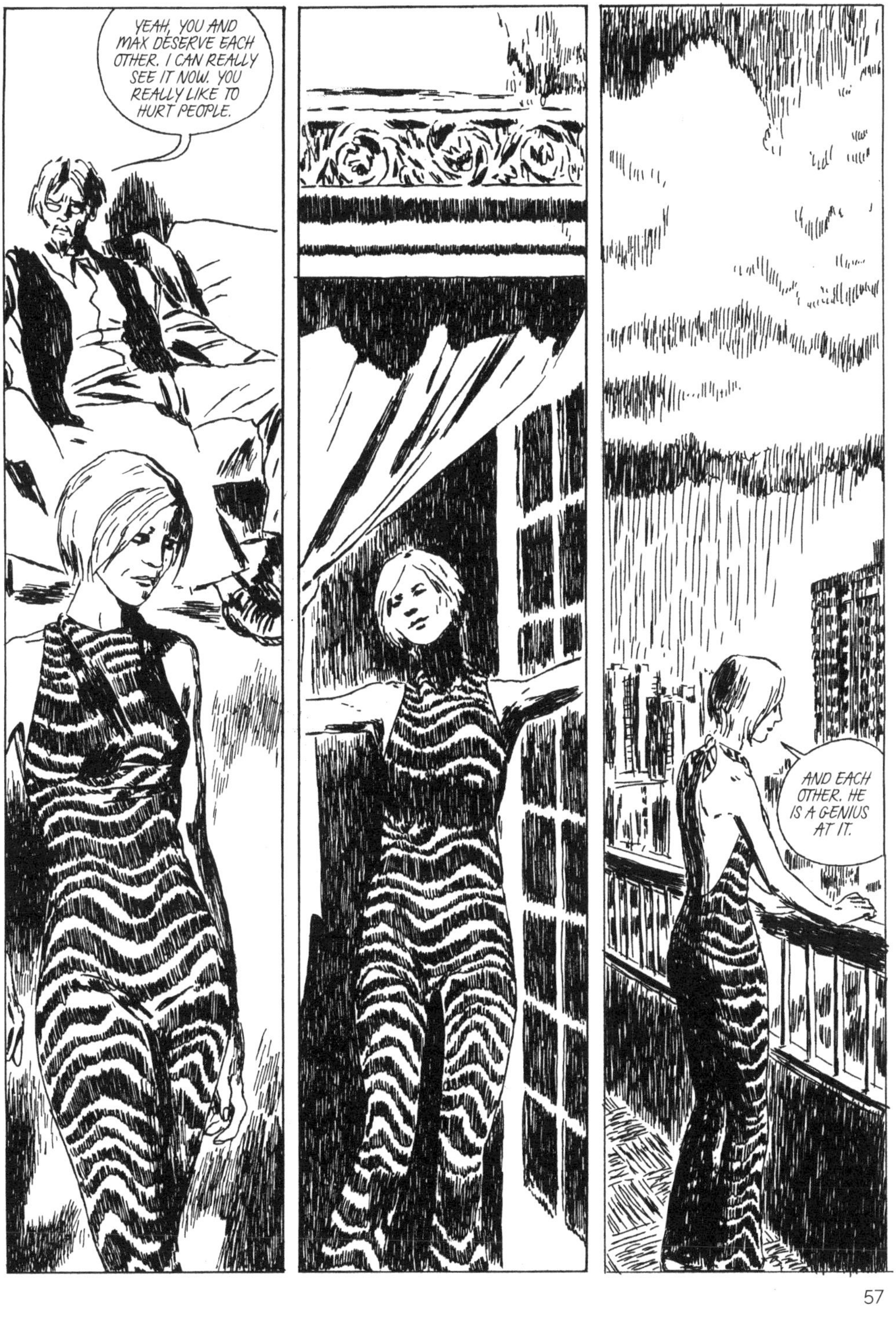
YEAH, YOU AND MAX DESERVE EACH OTHER. I CAN REALLY SEE IT NOW. YOU REALLY LIKE TO HURT PEOPLE.
AND EACH OTHER. HE IS A GENIUS AT IT.

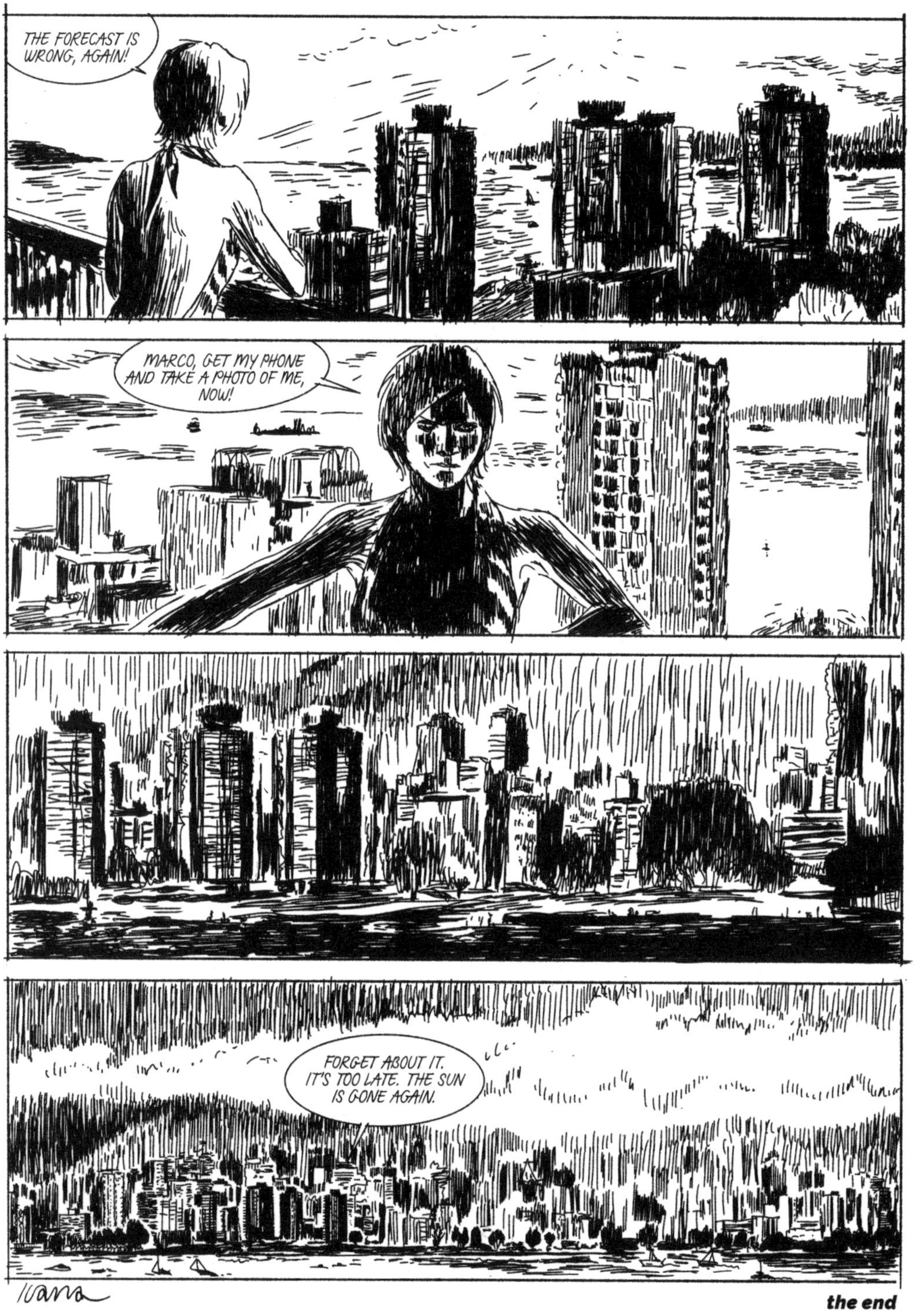
THE FORECAST IS WRONG, AGAIN!
MARCO, GET MY PHONE AND TAKE A PHOTO OF ME, NOW!
FORGET ABOUT IT. IT'S TOO LATE. THE SUN IS GONE AGAIN.

Ivana

the end

The original pages of this graphic novel lay abandoned for decades until Conundrum Press showed interest. This story is yours now. Make it your own. Read into it as much as you can.

Special thanks to the Canada Council for the Arts, Andy, Julian, Todd, Andrea and Chris.